Peaks and Plains by Rail

A guide to the routes, scenery and towns

Jarrold Colour Publications, Norwich

EDITOR'S INTRODUCTION

Contrast is the word which constantly springs to mind when describing the area covered by this book. There is the contrast between the mainly flat farmland of the Cheshire Plain and the craggy hills and dales of the Peak District. Within Cheshire and north Staffordshire there is everywhere the contrast between the rural and the industrial and between the ancient and the modern. Within the Peak District is the contrast between the bustling towns and the peace and solitude of the high places. This book will hopefully encourage the reader to explore the area and should give at least some idea of the most interesting places to visit.

Although the Peak District with its beauty spots, caverns and good walking country is an obvious attraction, Cheshire also has much to offer with historic Chester and an abundance of stately homes. There are interesting walks from Alderley Edge and Marple, and historic towns such as Knutsford and Nantwich have a distinctive character. This book also covers the northern part of Staffordshire including the Potteries and the town of Stafford itself. There is good rail access to several of the major attractions of the Potteries, including the most famous of all, the Wedgwood factory, and those who have never before alighted from the train at Stafford will be pleasantly surprised by its historic architecture.

Access to the Peak District by rail is hampered by the 'missing link' between Matlock and Buxton and PeakRail's efforts to rectify this short-sighted closure must be applauded and encouraged. Despite the loss of the direct access to Buxton from the south, its surviving link and the services to Glossop, New Mills and the stations along the Hope Valley line, particularly with its hourly stopping service from May 1989, do offer a number of alternatives for the tourist, the rambler and, 'Pacers' and 'Sprinters' permitting, the cyclist.

Famous names associated with this part of Britain include novelist Lewis Carroll, scientist Joseph Priestley, Prime Minister William Gladstone, car manufacturer Henry Royce, railway engineer Thomas Brassey, novelist Charlotte Brontë, author and angler Izaak Walton, the legendary Little John and even the French revolutionary Marat. It is possible to visit places connected with all of them. Fast modern trains will take you from most parts of the country to key junctions such as Crewe, Manchester, Stockport and Sheffield from where there are frequent local train services.

This book is in effect a second edition of *Cheshire and North Wales by Rail*, which was published in 1986, although a slightly different area is covered. North Wales has been omitted because the area is covered in the 1988 railguide *Wales and the Marches by Rail*. It was felt logical to include the Potteries and more of the Peak District to compensate for this, particularly as these areas had not been covered since the publication of *Five Shires by Rail* in 1986. I am indebted to the original authors of each of the sections for allowing me to re-use their work and for providing me with the information with which to update their previous contributions. Thanks are also due to Chris Jones for drawing the map and to the various photographers for allowing me to use their material.

If readers notice anything which is inaccurate or out of date we would be grateful if they could inform us so that this can be corrected in any future edition. Happy travelling!

Andrew Macfarlane
Knutsford
March 1989

CONTENTS

Front cover: Manchester–Hull train passing Buxworth, between New Mills and Chinley. (*Photo*: John Robinson)
Inside front cover: A 'Super Sprinter' approaching Cowburn Tunnel west of Edale. (*Photo*: Dr L. A. Nixon)
Title page: Steam returns to the Hope Valley as Class 8F No. 48151 leaves Edale with a Manchester–Derby enthusiasts' special train. (*Photo*: Tom Heavyside)
Back cover: The Gladstone Pottery Museum, Stoke-on-Trent.

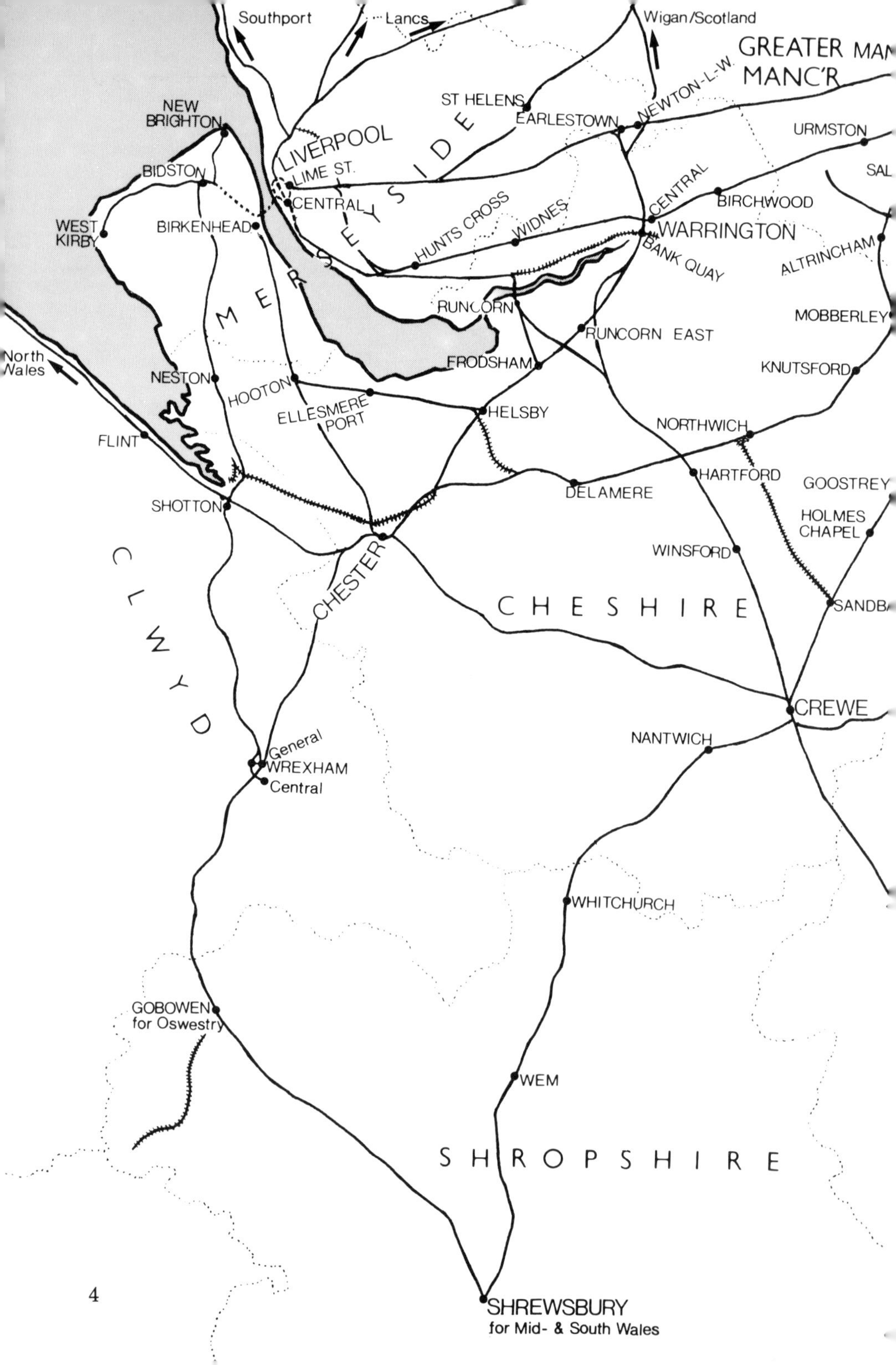

Southport
Lancs
Wigan/Scotland
GREATER MAN
MANC'R
ST HELENS
NEWTON-L-W.
EARLESTOWN
URMSTON
NEW BRIGHTON
LIVERPOOL
LIME ST.
CENTRAL
SAL
BIDSTON
CENTRAL
BIRCHWOOD
MERSEYSIDE
WARRINGTON
WEST KIRBY
BIRKENHEAD
HUNTS CROSS
WIDNES
BANK QUAY
ALTRINCHAM
MERSEY
RUNCORN
MOBBERLEY
RUNCORN EAST
North Wales
FRODSHAM
KNUTSFORD
NESTON
HOOTON
HELSBY
NORTHWICH
ELLESMERE PORT
DELAMERE
HARTFORD
GOOSTREY
FLINT
HOLMES CHAPEL
SHOTTON
WINSFORD
SANDB
CLWYD
CHESTER
CHESHIRE
CREWE
General
WREXHAM
Central
NANTWICH
WHITCHURCH
GOBOWEN
for Oswestry
WEM
SHROPSHIRE
SHREWSBURY
for Mid- & South Wales

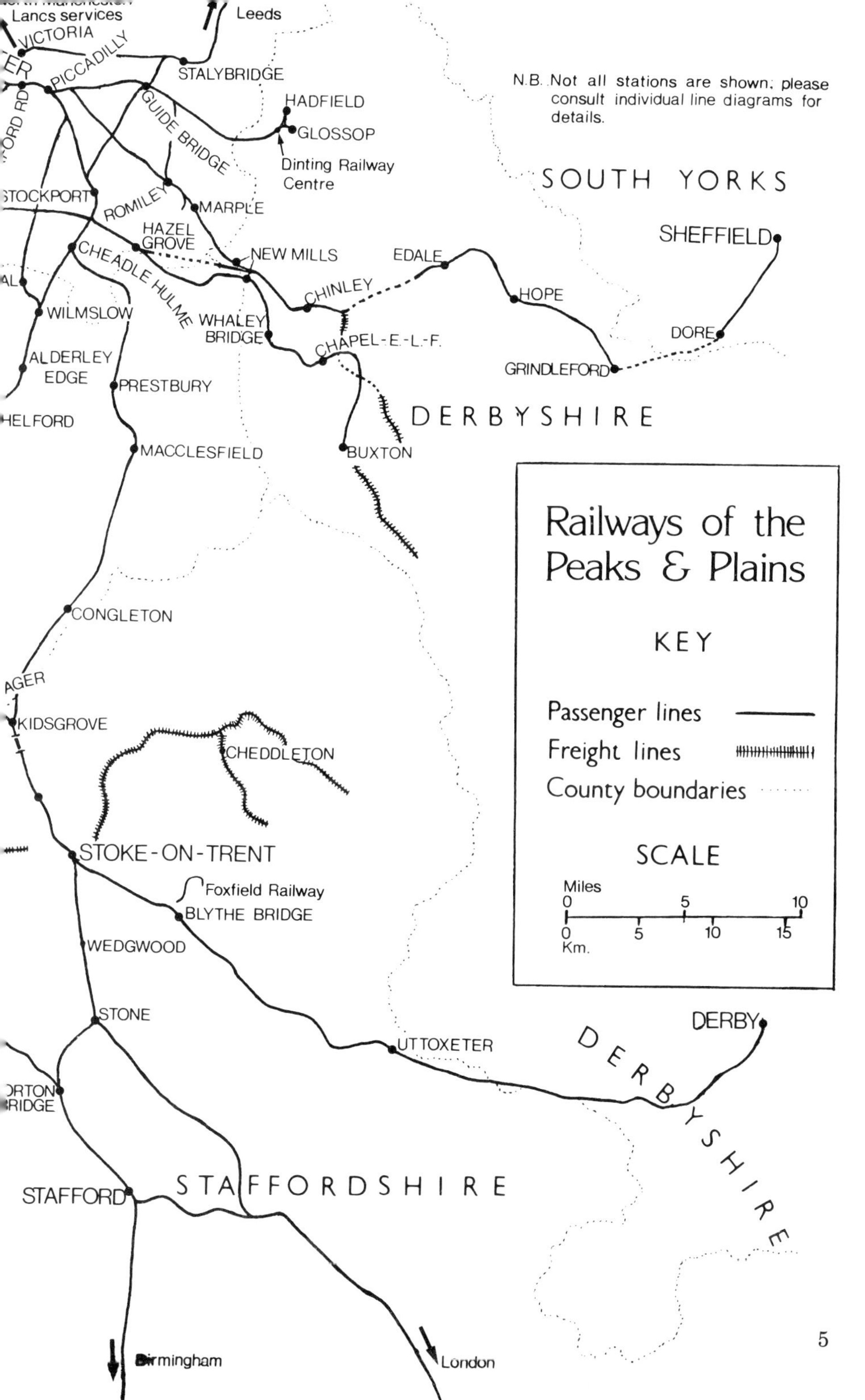

Lancs services
VICTORIA
Leeds
PICCADILLY
STALYBRIDGE
GUIDE BRIDGE
HADFIELD
GLOSSOP
Dinting Railway Centre
N.B. Not all stations are shown; please consult individual line diagrams for details.
SOUTH YORKS
STOCKPORT
ROMILEY
MARPLE
HAZEL GROVE
CHEADLE HULME
NEW MILLS
EDALE
SHEFFIELD
CHINLEY
HOPE
WILMSLOW
WHALEY BRIDGE
CHAPEL-E.-L.-F.
GRINDLEFORD
DORE
ALDERLEY EDGE
PRESTBURY
DERBYSHIRE
HELFORD
MACCLESFIELD
BUXTON
Railways of the Peaks & Plains
KEY
Passenger lines
Freight lines
County boundaries
CONGLETON
AGER
KIDSGROVE
CHEDDLETON
SCALE
Miles
0
5
10
0
5
10
15
Km.
STOKE-ON-TRENT
Foxfield Railway
BLYTHE BRIDGE
WEDGWOOD
STONE
UTTOXETER
DERBY
DERBYSHIRE
ORTON BRIDGE
STAFFORDSHIRE
STAFFORD
Birmingham
London

CREWE–LIVERPOOL
by Andrew Macfarlane

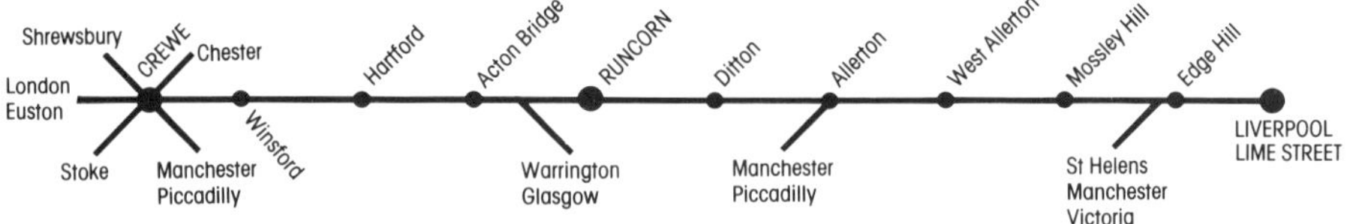

Crewe is a town which came into existence as a direct result of the 'Railway Mania'. Before the Grand Junction Railway came on the scene in 1837 there was only a small hamlet known as Church Coppenhall and the present town gets its name from Lord Crewe, whose family seat, Crewe Hall, lies a few miles to the east. The Grand Junction Railway's first line ran from Birmingham to Newton Junction (now Earlestown) on the Liverpool & Manchester Railway. Crewe became a junction with the opening of lines to Manchester and Holyhead and the Shrewsbury and Stoke lines followed later. The decision to site a locomotive works at Crewe led to a dramatic increase in the town's population in the latter half of the nineteenth century and the BREL works remains an important employer although Rolls-Royce now employ more people in their factory which produces the world's most exclusive car.

Our journey starts at one of the bay platforms at the north end of the station, usually platform 10. The station has undergone extensive modernisation in recent years although it retains much of its character. The local service from Crewe to Liverpool is basically hourly and this is supplemented by two-hourly Cardiff to Liverpool trains, all of which call at Runcorn and some at Hartford. InterCity services to Liverpool complete the picture, some of these trains calling at Crewe and/or Hartford on their way to Runcorn and Liverpool.

As we leave the station, on our immediate left is the new signalling centre, opened in 1985, and then the Crewe Heritage Centre which is based on the former Crewe North Junction signal-box in the 'V' of the Holyhead and Liverpool lines. The heritage centre was opened by Her Majesty the Queen in 1987 to coincide with the 150th anniversary of the arrival of the railway in Crewe. In 1989 it will be the base for steam locomotives operating along the North Wales coast and to Shrewsbury and Hereford. The northbound or 'down' Liverpool independent line rises to join us to our left as our train gathers speed. The independent lines, as their name suggests, provide an alternative route for freight trains avoiding the passenger station and could well be vitally important if railborne freight traffic mushrooms with the opening of the Channel Tunnel.

New housing is encroaching further northwards alongside our route and there could be a case for a new station on this section in years to come. We enter open country and our route is four-track until just south of **Winsford** Station ($7\frac{1}{2}$ miles from Crewe). The station is well-used despite being some distance from the town it is intended to serve. The town of Winsford developed mainly as a result of salt mining. It was formerly two towns, Over and Wharton, which were amalgamated to form one urban district in the 1880s. The name Winsford was chosen as a neutral one. It is interesting to note that, a century later, British Rail still use the name Over & Wharton for the terminus of the salt branch from Winsford Junction. The town of Winsford has grown considerably since the war with overspill housing development from Liverpool and a new industrial estate. In the process it has lost much of its character although some nineteenth century timber public houses survive near the bridge over the Weaver.

South of our next stop, **Hartford**, the line crosses the Weaver Navigation by the substantial Vale Royal viaduct. Hartford Station serves a mainly residential area and is a railhead for Northwich. Since May 1988 the station has enjoyed an improved service of InterCity trains to London and to holiday resorts on the south coast. Greenbank Station on the Manchester–Chester line is 20 minutes' walk away (turn right at the top of the approach road). North of Hartford we pass under this line and a freight-only connecting spur trails in to our right at Hartford LNW Junction which boasts a London & North Western Railway signal-box on the west side of the line. We are soon at **Acton Bridge** station. Cyclists will find this a good starting point from which to explore some of the lanes of Cheshire. They will discover that it is not all flat as its reputation might imply!

The listed Dutton viaduct takes us over the Weaver Navigation, the scene of a collision between two freight trains in 1975, one carrying whisky and the other (caustic) soda! There is a proposal to build a new InterCity 'park and ride' station near this point to provide a convenient interchange with the M56 motorway. At Weaver Junction we part company with the main line to Glasgow by means of a flying junction, the first to be installed in Britain. Soon we are surrounded by the regimented housing of Runcorn New Town and at Halton Junction a freight-only spur from Frodsham Junction on the Warrington–Chester line trails is on our left. This spur is used by a summer Saturdays Liverpool to Llandudno train.

We arrive at **Runcorn** Station, the most important on this section of line. A branch line descends to our left to serve the complex of ICI works. Runcorn Station serves the 'old' town which has a pleasant traditional shopping area straddling the Bridgewater Canal, which joins the Mersey at this point having wound its way across the Cheshire Plain from Worsley near Manchester. The new town of Runcorn is two miles away and has a modern shopping centre known as 'Shopping City' and a unique network of busways which link the outlying parts of the new town with the centre. One of the local buses connects Runcorn Station with a park in the heart of the new town. Here there is a dry ski slope and other sports facilities and, of perhaps greater interest, the excavated remains of Norton Priory.

The Augustinian priory was built as the prosperous abode for 24 canons in

Lion, originally built in 1838 for the Liverpool & Manchester Railway, attracts plenty of attention at the Crewe Rail Heritage Centre in the summer of 1987. (*Photo*: Tom Heavyside)

1134. The building was transformed into a Tudor and later a Georgian mansion before being abandoned in 1921. Today the site has a prize-winning museum on life in twelfth-century Cheshire and some beautiful gardens. The remains of the priory include the foundations of the church and cloistral buildings. One of the undercrofts has a fine Norman doorway, and arcading which was found behind the brickwork of a later house has been lovingly restored. Stone coffins with carved lids and medieval tiled floors can be seen in the adjoining museum. The gardens have features such as a laburnum arch and a stream glade with azaleas and rhododendrons, and close by is an authentic eighteenth-century walled garden. Age-old crafts and artforms such as tile-making, sculpture and carving are revived and celebrated in regular workshops, exhibitions and demonstrations. The priory is open from March to October from 12 noon until 5 p.m. (6 p.m. on bank holidays and at weekends) and from 12 noon to 4 p.m. from November to February, although the walled garden is closed between these months. The later history of Runcorn is documented in the Shaw museum. Interestingly, the town was once a health resort known as Montpelier, although this is hard to imagine nowadays with the large number of chemical plants in the area.

After leaving Runcorn our train crosses the Mersey estuary and the Manchester Ship Canal by means of the massive Runcorn Bridge. Note the castle-like towers at either end which recalls the fact that Aethelfleda had a castle where its foundations stand. There is a good view of the adjacent Runcorn–Widnes Road Bridge with its graceful single arch, with a span of 1,082 feet, and its roadway suspended on metal cables. **Ditton** Station, formerly Ditton Junction, is situated in a mainly industrial area and is served only during peak periods. Here a freight-only line from Warrington joins us and we note the British Oxygen plant to our left from which many trainloads of liquified gas leave each year to destinations all over the country. Further along on our left the giant Ford factory at Halewood is also rail-served. We may see overhead an aircraft heading to Speke Airport, which has been growing in importance in recent years. A new terminal building was opened in 1986 to replace the 1930s building which is visible from the line. Nearby is Speke Hall, a fine half-timbered Tudor manor house which is open to the public and well worth a visit. Merseybus services run from Garston Station on the Northern line of Merseyrail to Speke village, a mile from the hall.

At Speke Junction we will see large numbers of wagons of coal awaiting export to Ireland and the Isle of Man from Garston Dock. Before Allerton we pass over the Northern line, the former Cheshire Lines Committee route into Liverpool, which was fully reopened in 1983 after eleven years of closure to passengers. At Allerton Junction we are joined from the right by the line from Manchester Piccadilly via Warrington. **Allerton, West Allerton** and **Mossley Hill** stations serve the suburbs of Liverpool. At **Edge Hill**, we join the line from Manchester Victoria, the original Liverpool & Manchester Railway opened in 1830. The buildings of Edge Hill Station were restored in connection with the 150th anniversary celebrations of the line in 1980. Beyond Edge Hill the line enters Lime Street cutting, an awe-inspiring nineteenth-century engineering achievement. Note the names of the streets above affixed to the cutting side. **Lime Street** Station, now the principal one in Liverpool, was extensively modernised in the mid-1980s and the concourse enlarged. This now presents a light and airy appearance. Beneath the main station is Lime Street Low Level Station on the Liverpool Loop line with frequent services to destinations in Wirral.

Liverpool, famous for its two cathedrals, its ferries, its football clubs and the Beatles, is well worth spending some time in, the sense of humour of its inhabitants being well known. A short distance from Lime Street Station is the Walker Art Gallery and Liverpool City Museum in William Brown Street. Exhibits in the gallery include the famous *When did you last see your father?*, and the City Museum has galleries dealing with prehistoric life, local history and the arts as well as having its own aquarium.

CREWE–CHESTER
by David Roberts

Travellers from **Crewe** to Chester will either be on through service to North Wales and Holyhead (for the Irish ferry) or will board the diesel multiple-unit (nowadays often a 'Sprinter' unit) shuttle normally resting at bay platform 9. This is the main access route from the south and east to seaside resorts such as Rhyl, Prestatyn and Llandudno. 1989 will see the regular operation of steam-hauled trains from Crewe to Chester and onwards to North Wales and Shrewsbury.

We leave the station, bearing left, leaving the West Coast main line and soon pass Crewe locomotive works on the right-hand side, before running into a shallow cutting. The London & North Western Railway Crewe Steel Works signal-box is to our left, reminding us that the company known as the 'Premier line' made its own steel in the town. After passing the suburbs, the train emerges into open country, immediately crossing over a large stream. This is the River Weaver, meandering north towards Northwich.

About five miles from Crewe, the Middlewich branch of the Shropshire Union Canal approaches on the right and crosses underneath to join the main canal on the left where a barge marina can be seen. The skeletal shape of a radio telescope may also be glimpsed. This is controlled by radio-link with the famous Jodrell Bank telescope which lies sixteen miles to the north-east. Modern cheese warehouses and a coal depot mark the hamlet of Calveley. Trains used to stop here to unload goods for the canal which now passes under the line again and appears at Bunbury locks on the right. The 'Shroppie' now runs alongside us virtually the rest of the way to Chester.

On the left, we look out over the Cheshire Plain, an area predominantly used for dairy farming and grazing. Small pastures abound, although here and there trees stagger oddly across larger fields, marking where hedges once stood. Some of the farms show a prosperous past with their well-built buildings with tall chimneys, leaded-paned windows and diaper patterns in their brickwork. We pass the platforms of the closed station of Beeston Castle & Tarporley which Cheshire County Council is keen to reopen, and to our right is another LNWR signal-box controlling the only semaphore signalling on the line. To our left is a former oil storage facility built into the hillside.

In the distance to the left can be seen the steep, wooded sandstone outcrops of the Peckforton and Bickerton Hills. The remains of Beeston Castle can be seen nearest us and behind it is the more substantial Peckforton 'Castle'. Beeston Castle was built by Ranulf the Third, Earl of Chester, in the 1220s. Ranulf was an independent Norman earl and, unlike most of his fellow barons, loyal to King John, so the castle was designed to face invasions from both England and Wales. The castle was partly destroyed after the Civil War. Peckforton Castle was designed for the Tollemache family in 1844 in the style of a medieval castle and until recently was their main seat.

The line gently curves to the right, passing the site of Tattenhall Road Station

where, on the left, a pub stands. On the same side, a mile further on, a few yards
of overgrown trackbed are all that remain of the fifteen mile branch line running
from Chester south to Whitchurch. We enter a cutting for about a mile now before
emerging near the village of Rowton on the right. In 1645, during the Civil War,
Chester had come under siege from Parliamentarian forces, and King Charles I
marched into the city to muster an army for its relief. On the 24 September, he
watched from the city walls and saw his Royalist army defeated at the Battle of
Rowton Heath. Over 600 men were killed on both sides. We pass Waverton,
another potential site for a new station.

For the last mile or so the train runs through a cutting before slowing down
and emerging with the line from Manchester joining from the right. We pass the
power signal-box on the same side and run into **Chester** Station. Passengers
either carry on through to North Wales and Holyhead or change for Liverpool
and Wirral, Shrewsbury or Manchester. The city centre is about a fifteen minute
walk away. Go down City Road (directly opposite the station forecourt) and take
the subway at the end to Foregate Street (which starts on the right across the
large traffic island). The main shopping area is ahead. A frequent and cheap bus
service is run by Chester City Transport from the station forecourt to the Town
Hall.

CREWE–SHREWSBURY

by David Latimer

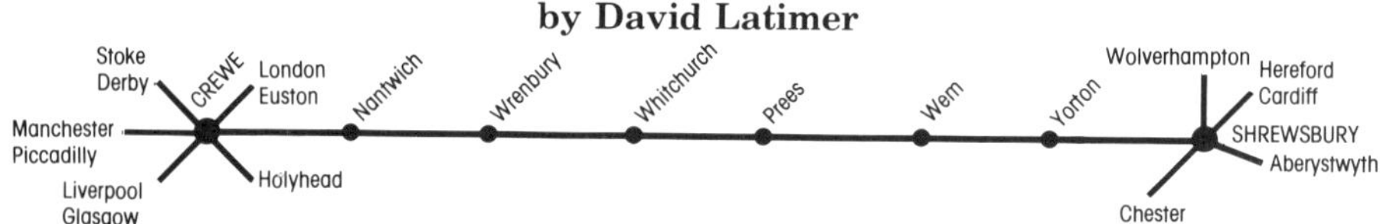

Crewe may not have the attractions that the town at the other end of this line –
Shrewsbury – may have, but it is nonetheless an interesting town, boasting
Queens Park, one of the finest municipal parks in Britain with magnificent
landscaped gardens and woodland. The park was donated to the borough by the
former London & North Western Railway Company, who built it to block the
proposed route into the town by a rival railway company, the Great Western
Railway. Unfortunately, the park is a fair hike from the railway station, so only
those with a couple of hours to spare between trains are advised to walk there,
but there is a bus service from the bus station. The main shopping centre and bus
station is also a good walk from the station, but frequent buses leave the station
forecourt to the town centre. The shopping district is spacious and well-planned
and boasts some well-known big stores. Those not ambitious enough to venture
into town and feeling thirsty will not be disappointed by strolling down Nantwich
Road, on which the station is situated. Here will be found an array of very smart
and interesting pubs to suit all tastes.

And so back to your train to Shrewsbury! The fast trains on the Crewe–
Shrewsbury line are essentially part of the Liverpool and Manchester to Cardiff
'Sprinter Express' service inaugurated in May 1988 and there is an hourly service
from Crewe to the Welsh capital. It should be remembered, however, that these
longer distance services do not call at intermediate stations between Crewe and
Shrewsbury. Local trains run at approximately two-hourly intervals. On leaving
Crewe, Shrewsbury trains depart from the West Coast Main Line just outside the
station and head south-west, past an array of sidings which soon give way to a
brief glimpse of the Cheshire countryside. The train passes through Crewe's
suburban village of Willaston, where there are hopes that the village local station
will be reopened for the benefit of local residents in the not too distant future.

About four and a half miles out of Crewe, the train pulls into the small medieval market town of **Nantwich**. This town is well worth exploring. It has a fascinating fourteenth-century church, a museum, historic buildings and other tourist attractions. Nantwich is often described as a 'mini Chester' and one often gets that feeling walking down its narrow streets with their quaint shops, pubs and historic buildings. Like Chester, however it has its parking problems, especially on market days when a place to park can be impossible to find, so what better way to visit than by train? Not all trains call at this unmanned station, however, and the station is closed on Sundays, so intending visitors are warned not to hop on any Shrewsbury train without checking the timetable first. On leaving Nantwich the train passes over the River Weaver and just a little further after this on the left is the point where the old line to Market Drayton, now closed for many years, once left our line. Another half mile and our line crosses the Shropshire Union Canal which links the Black Country with the Mersey Estuary at Ellesmere Port. No longer used by commercial traffic, this canal is now very popular with the holiday cruisers.

The railway continues through undulating countryside to the small but well-kept halt at the tiny village of **Wrenbury**. Here the line passes close to the famed Llangollen Canal, a branch of the Shropshire Union Canal and within walking distance of the station. Wrenbury is a pretty village with several half-timbered buildings and a pub. The drawbridge over the canal is an attractive feature. About halfway between Wrenbury and Whitchurch the line passes over into the county of Shropshire, a rural county which once bore witness to many border skirmishes between English and Welsh. **Whitchurch** is the next station. Once very busy as a junction for services to Oswestry, it has now settled down to a slower pace but is still well patronised by the locals.

This interesting little market town, although inheriting a different style of architecture to that of Nantwich, is equally quaint but perhaps a little quieter. It has several Georgian buildings, an almshouse and good shops that one doesn't have to do battle with cars and crowds to reach. The town is famed locally as being the birthplace of the composer Sir Edward German.

The next station – or halt – is **Prees**, which is actually about a mile from the little village it serves. Beyond Prees the countryside gets a bit more interesting with a few proper hills breaking up the previous undulation. Three more miles see the railway reach the little town of **Wem**, perhaps best known for its brewery. The Wem Brewery is now part of the Greenall Whitley empire, but it still has its distinctive brew and the beer can be purchased throughout Shropshire and Cheshire. The station at Wem is basic but neat and particularly well used by local folk.

After leaving Wem the line continues southwards towards Shrewsbury, passing the little station at **Yorton**. The former signal-box from here is now at Arley station on the Severn Valley Railway. We enter the northern industrial outskirts of Shrewsbury, passing the signal box at Harlescott level-crossing to our right. As the train approaches **Shrewsbury** station it becomes obvious that it is a fairly important railway junction. In fact this station is the interchange point of six routes – the line to the Cambrian Coast, the Central Wales line, the line on to South Wales via Hereford, the line to Wolverhampton, that to Chester and of course our line from Crewe. The other lines converging on Shrewsbury are fully described in our companion volume, *Wales and the Marches by Rail*.

Shrewsbury, situated on the River Severn, is the county town of Shropshire and could justifiably claim a chapter all to itself. It is a picturesque and historic market town of some size and boasts some fine old buildings which include the eleventh-century red sandstone castle restored by Telford and now owned by the local council. There are also two ancient bridges and a large number of half-timbered buildings. Being a border town, Shrewsbury saw a number of bloody skirmishes – hence its castle. Indeed its early importance was due to its key position on roads into Wales, centuries before the railway came. Today the town, as well as being a stopping-off point for tourists, is equally acclaimed for its excellent shopping facilities, which are all near the station.

The station itself is also worth a mention. It is a fine old building with a charm all of its own and has been further enhanced by recent superb renovation. The main station building fronts onto a small square in the centre of the town and doesn't look unlike a modest stately home.

The Crewe–Shrewsbury line cannot lay claim to the magnificent scenery that other lines to Shrewsbury can, such as those from the Cambrian Coast and Central Wales, but its route is fairly pleasant and essentially rural and more importantly it does pass through historic towns on its route. In fact it is an ideal route for those touring Wales and The Marches by rail for it links the two key junctions of the region – Crewe and Shrewsbury.

CREWE–STOKE-ON-TRENT

by Basil Jeuda

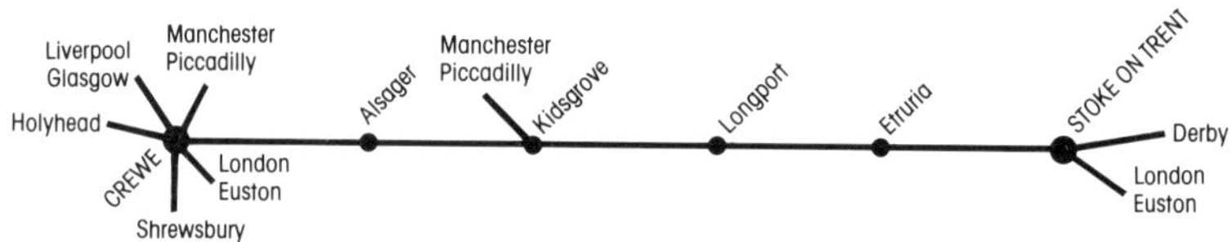

The line that runs from Crewe to Stoke was part of the former North Staffordshire Railway, whose lines radiated out from Stoke-on-Trent. The important parts of the North Staffordshire Railway in terms of their links with other railway systems were very largely completed and opened by 1849.

The journey from **Crewe** will probably start at platform 4 which was refurbished as part of the modernisation programme carried out in the summer of 1985. The service to Stoke is provided by 'Sprinter' diesel units and is basically hourly, running through to Derby. Some trains start back from North Wales and use through platform 5 at Crewe. On the right-hand side can be seen some creamy-yellow brickwork and some fairly ornate brick arches and this can be identified as part of the original Crewe station. As the train departs, almost immediately on the left-hand side you will see the now redundant Crewe South Junction signal-box which was built in the 1930s to a standard London Midland & Scottish Railway design; it was taken out of use during the modernisation of 1985. The line veers away from the main line to the south and on the left you can see the Midland Rollmakers building, and here starts the journey proper along the former NSR line to Stoke.

The journey shortly becomes single track for a few miles and we pass under the new link road from the M6 to Crewe. After about a mile or so can be seen the beautifully designed North Staffordshire crossing house at Barthomley on the left; there are very few houses of this type which have survived and this one, which was built around 1850, is particularly impressive. About a mile or so after that you will pass under the M6 motorway and then shortly reach a level-crossing at Radway Green. All that is left of the former station are the passenger platforms. Beyond the station to the right can be seen the sidings connection to the Radway Green armaments factory.

A mile or so further on, **Alsager** town is reached and just before the station is a busy level-crossing, monitored by closed-circuit television from the Crewe signalling centre. Alsager Station (unstaffed) is in a state of disrepair but the station house on the right is a very fine example of a NSR station building; look particularly at the ornate weather boards. About a mile after leaving Alsager can be seen trailing in from the left-hand side a railway cutting at the former Lawton Junction, which linked our line with the London & North Western main line from Crewe to Manchester at Sandbach. This line, once very busy with coal traffic, closed in the early 1970s. Also coming in on the left-hand side can be seen the Trent & Mersey Canal which runs parallel with the railway as far as **Kidsgrove**.

Kidsgrove Station, formerly known as Harecastle, is an important junction with the main line from Manchester. In former years, it was an even more important junction station, linking up with the Audley line and with the line to Sandbach and, by changing railway stations, the loop line which one joined at the original Kidsgrove station, a quarter of a mile to the north. There is very little left of the original Harecastle station but the waiting room on the platform from Crewe to Stoke contains some original architecture. The footbridge is a standard North Staffordshire Railway footbridge, and, looking across to the coal yard, one can see the red and blue brick-built weighing office.

On leaving Kidsgrove station, you pass the modern signal-box and cross over the Trent & Mersey Canal. If you look right, you can see the twin canal tunnels of the Harecastle Tunnel, one built by James Brindley and the other by Thomas Telford, with the original tunnel on the left-hand side. Only the later Telford bore remains in use. You will now enter the 'new' tunnel at Harecastle, built with electrification in the 1960s, with the original, much longer tunnel on the left-hand side. The three original Harecastle tunnels proved a major obstacle during electrification of the Stoke–Macclesfield line in the 1960s and a $2\frac{1}{2}$ mile deviation had to be built to the west, opening in June 1966. On leaving the tunnel, on the left-hand side you can see a modest embankment on which ran the line into the old Harecastle tunnel, and on the right-hand side can be seen the winding engine house of the old Chatterley ironworks. We now commence the run-in through Trent Vale into Stoke-on-Trent and there is a fair degree of industrial activity to be seen on both sides of the line. The NSR Bradwell Sidings signal-box is passed on the right-hand side and Longport Junction is reached, where the LMS signal-box can be seen to the right.

Longport goods shed on the left-hand side is an original one, brick-built, to which has been added a robust timber-framed building. As you stop at Longport Station, look at the brick lattice work in the station construction and in the gable end. You can also see some of the original tiling on the roof of the passenger station. As you leave Longport, on the left-hand side shortly will come into view Middleport Pottery and soon after that you can see in the distance the site of the 1986 National Garden Festival. The BR-built Grange Junction signal-box is passed on the right-hand side, and on the left is Shelton steelworks, now reduced to a rolling mill only.

On the right-hand side shortly is passed the site of the former Wolstanton colliery, closed in 1985. Shelton steelworks comes more closely into view on the left-hand side and you can see some wagons of steel bar alongside the works. What looks like a footpath trails in from the left and this is the track bed of the former Loop line, and immediately after that you arrive at the island platform of **Etruria** Station. On the far left can be seen the skyline of Hanley and the parish church of Etruria. On the right-hand side we pass various pottery factories. We shortly reach, on the left-hand side, the former Cockshute sidings, which was an important interchange with the Trent & Mersey Canal which can be seen coming in on the left and passing underneath the line. On the right-hand side can be seen the carriage sheds which date back to North Staffordshire Railway times.

The Cliffe Vale sidings of the English China Clay Company, served by block trains from Cornwall, can be seen on the right-hand side as we approach **Stoke** Station, $14\frac{3}{4}$ miles from Crewe. As we pass the power signal-box and enter the station, on the left-hand side are the buildings of the North Staffordshire Polytechnic, and immediately beyond that the North Stafford Hotel, built in 1848, which is a listed building and has very prominent lattice brickwork. Such brickwork can also be seen in Stoke station and the station design is similar, in terms of door lintels in particular, to that seen at Longport and at Alsager. For more information on Stoke please see page 57.

STOKE–STAFFORD

by Andrew Macfarlane

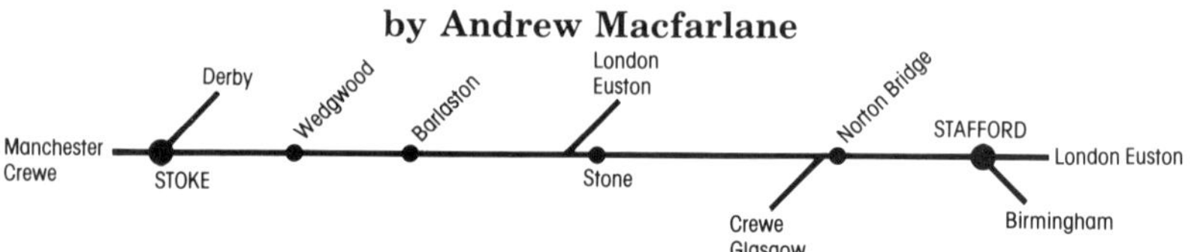

Our journey begins under the overall roof of the Potteries' main railhead, once the focal point of the North Staffordshire Railway or, more familiarly, the 'Knotty'. Fast trains from **Stoke** to Stafford run at approximately hourly intervals, forming a section of the InterCity service from Manchester Piccadilly to Birmingham New Street. Local trains run at more irregular intervals and call at all stations.

As we leave Stoke, two lines diverge to our left. The left-hand, single-track route is the freight-only Churnet Valley line to Oakamoor and Caldon Low which is currently 'mothballed' pending possible future use. The North Staffordshire Railway preservation site is at the former Cheddleton station on the Oakamoor line and there is a possibility that the line between Cheddleton and Oakamoor, and even the section beyond to Alton, of Towers fame, may be reopened for summer tourist trains in the future. The right-hand, double-track line is the route to Derby described elsewhere in this book.

To our right now is the wagon repair works of Rail Car Services. A branch line once diverged to our right before the former Trentham station to serve Trentham Gardens, a very popular tourist attraction. If only that line were still open today! To our left is Hem Heath Colliery which provides a considerable amount of coal traffic for British Rail in the shape of 'merry-go-round' trains to Fiddlers Ferry, Ironbridge and Rugeley power stations. Next of interest to our left is the **Wedgwood** factory and we pass over the level-crossing to call at the station which carries the famous name. The next stop, after only a short distance, is **Barlaston**. The seventeenth-century Barlaston Hall is now an Adult College.

After another couple of miles we pass the former Meaford Power Station to our right. One of the steam engines which used to shunt the sidings here is now preserved on the East Lancashire Railway at Bury. Just before **Stone** Station we have a choice of routes. Straight on is the direct line to Colwich Junction on the West Coast Main Line, which is used by trains from Manchester to London which do not call at Stafford. To the right is the line to Norton Bridge, used by Birmingham trains and by the local service to Stafford. Stone Station only has platforms on the Norton Bridge line. Note the fine North Staffordshire Railway building to our left. Stone is noted as the birthplace of the painter Peter de Wint (1784–1849) and of the poet Richard Barnfield, a contemporary of Shakespeare. The Earl of St Vincent, the great naval commander, one of whose junior officers was Nelson, is buried in the churchyard here.

We now travel through a mainly agricultural landscape to join the West Coast Main Line immediately before **Norton Bridge** Station, an island platform. Close to the station, at Shallowford, is the farm of Halfhead, bequeathed by Izaak Walton to the town of Stafford but since sold. The half-timbered cottage where he was born is preserved as a Walton memorial and is open from 10 a.m. to 4 p.m. daily except Tuesday. Three miles to the west is Eccleshall, where there are the remains of a castle of the bishops of Lichfield and a fine Early English church. The William and Mary Mansion House built among the castle ruins and incorporating some of its walls is open to the public on Sundays, Mondays, Tuesdays and bank holidays from June to September, and on Sundays and bank holidays only from Easter to early October, from 2 p.m. to 5.30 p.m. There is a nature trail in the twenty acres of wooded grounds, which include an unusual nine-sided tower and a medieval bridge across the moat.

We pass the modern Norton Bridge signal-box to our left and the countryside becomes flatter as we approach Stafford. As we pass under the M6 motorway note the castle on the hilltop to our right. The former Great Northern Railway line from Derby once joined from our left and the London & North Western Railway line from Shrewsbury from the right, behind the Universal Grinding Wheel factory. Stafford no. 5 signal-box is also to our right, still with a mechanical lever frame. As we come to a stand in the 1960s **Stafford** Station, the former steam locomotive depot is to our right, recently converted for industrial use.

Stafford is the ancient county town of Staffordshire and was the birthplace of Izaak Walton (1593–1683), the genial author of *The Compleat Angler*. Its traditional staple industry was bootmaking and this is referred to in Sheridan's famous toast, 'May the trade of Stafford be trod under foot by all the world'. Electrical and structural engineering industries are now major employers in the town. The large and handsome parish church of St Mary's contains a bust of Izaak Walton, who was baptised in the remarkable Norman font. Outside the west end of the church are the foundations of St Bertelin's Chapel, dating from around the year 1000, which were excavated in 1954, and there is a replica of the wooden Saxon cross which lies buried beneath. St Bertelin was a Mercian prince who established a hermitage in Stafford. The parish church has an unusual octagonal tower, the foundations of which date from the 1220s, and the doorway to the north transept dates from the fourteenth century.

The origins of the town of Stafford date back to the Mercian kingdom of the 700s. The town has associations with Henry VII, who stayed here on the way to the Battle of Bosworth in 1485 and Queen Elizabeth I who visited the town and accepted the gift of a silver cup from its citizens. The Irish-born dramatist R. B. Sheridan, author of *The Rivals*, was M.P. for Stafford from 1780 to 1806. In Greengate Street there are a number of fine old buildings, including the half-timbered High House, built in 1595, where Charles I and Prince Rupert were lodged in 1642. The building is the largest timber-framed town house in England and now contains a Heritage Exhibition and Tourist Information Centre. The house and exhibition are open from 10 a.m. to 5 p.m. on Monday to Friday and from 9 a.m. to 12.30 p.m. on Saturdays. The tourist information centre is open from 9 a.m. to 5 p.m. on Monday to Friday and from 9 a.m. to 12.30 p.m. on Saturdays. Also in Greengate Street is the Swan Hotel, at which George Borrow was ostler in 1825, and the Post Office, formerly Chetwynd House, occupied by the Duke of Cumberland in 1745 and later by Sheridan. The William Salt Library, 19 Eastgate Street, is a beautiful eighteenth-century house containing a valuable collection of books and manuscripts relating to Staffordshire and is open from Tuesday to Friday from 10 a.m. to 5 p.m.

CREWE–STAFFORD

by Geoffrey Wyatt

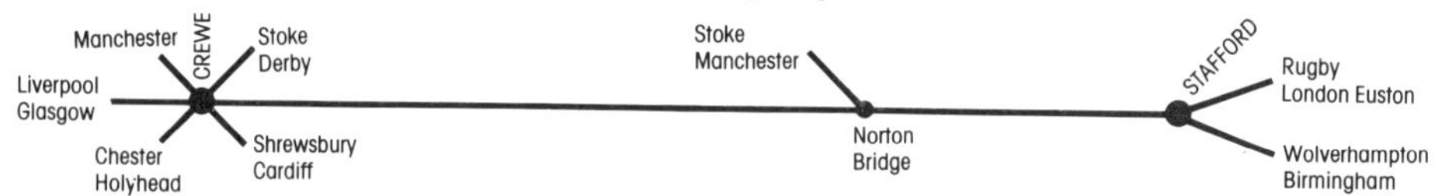

Crewe owes its existence to the railway and is world famous for its junction, works and locomotives. It is also home to Chester Barrie clothing, Co-op 99 tea, the Wellcome Foundation and Rolls Royce cars.

Trains from Crewe to Stafford form part of the main InterCity service to the south. We leave **Crewe**, passing the locomotive holding sidings and diesel depot on the right, also the line diverging towards Shrewsbury. To the left is the former South Junction signal-box, the line to Kidsgrove and the carriage shed. To the right lie the Basford Hall marshalling yards with their 150 ft-high lighting towers. The yards are $1\frac{3}{4}$ miles long, stretching to Basford Hall Junction, where the independent lines, which run along the other side of the yards, join the main lines.

We pass beneath a minor road bridge and pass Betley Road signal-box and railway cottages to the left. The Cheshire/Staffordshire border runs parallel for about a mile before crossing the line. The scenery consists of rolling hills with trees and copses here and there and the line affords several panoramic views. The train runs through Madeley cuttings to pass Madeley signal-box and Nether Hey Lane Industrial Estate on the left. On the right are the banked sides of Madeley reservoir, marked at the north end by a lifebelt. The railway diverging right joins the former Stoke to Market Drayton line which will soon pass above our train. The line now serves only the collieries of Silverdale and Holditch. We pass under the A53 road and see on the right the banks of Whitmore reservoir, also distinguished by a lifebelt at its north end. Both reservoirs were built by the London & North Western Railway and still supply water to Crewe. Until 1965 Whitmore reservoir supplied water to the former Whitmore water troughs where steam locomotives could replenish their tenders at speed.

On the right of the line is the black and white fronted Cock Inn public house on the A51, which crosses the line before running parallel to it for about a mile. We can now see the impressive Hatton pumping station with a tall chimney, built

Southbound 'Speedlink' freight train passing Madeley on the West Coast Main Line *en route* from Speke to Dagenham Dock. The West Coast Main Line should see an increase in its freight traffic with the opening of the Channel Tunnel. (*Photo*: John Robinson)

at the end of the last century. As the A51 veers left a minor road runs from it parallel to the line for about 1½ miles. We can now seen the Millmeece pumping station. Built of red brick to a more modern design than the one at Hatton, it also boasts a tall chimney.

Soon after this, if your train is on the fast line (the left hand line), you may detect a slight brake application as the train slows down to ninety miles an hour for the junction at **Norton Bridge** where the line from Stoke-on-Trent converges. Norton Bridge is the only station between Crewe and Stafford to retain its train service, but all trains run to or from Stoke. The station is an island platform with the southbound (up) fast line to the east and four others to the west. The black and white Izaak Walton cottage and museum which was donated to the town of Stafford for charitable purposes may be glimpsed on the left.

As we approach Stafford – and passing under the M6 motorway we are only 1¾ miles away – the scenery becomes flatter. The land on either side of the train is marshy and prone to flooding. Stafford Castle stands on high ground about a mile to the right. We shall soon pass Henry Venables' timber yard on our left which supplied timber for repairs to York Minster. The former line left of the yard was the Great Northern Railway line to Uttoxeter. With foresight in the 1960s this and the North Staffordshire Railway Uttoxeter–Alton line could have been part of a direct link from the West Midlands to the popular Alton Towers. On the right is the Universal Grinding Wheel Company and GEC Castle Engineering Works with part of the Stafford to Market Drayton line still used as a siding. We now arrive at **Stafford** station, rebuilt in 1961/2 under the Euston to Liverpool and Manchester electrification project. For more details on the town of Stafford please see the end of the section on Stoke to Stafford.

STOKE–DERBY

by Tim Young

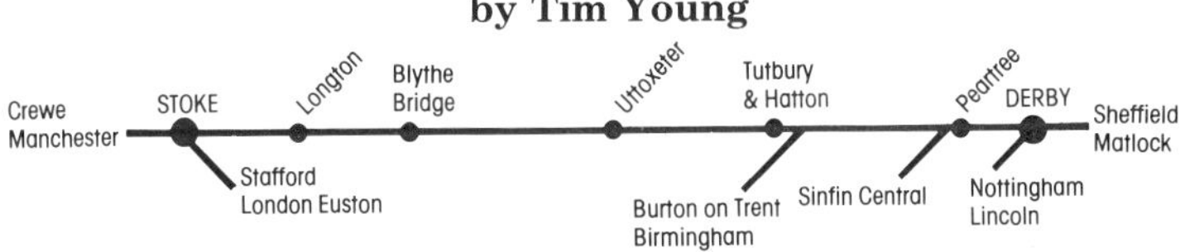

Trains from Stoke to Derby are a continuation of the service from Crewe and are usually formed of 'Sprinter' units running approximately every hour. As we leave **Stoke** station, the four floodlight pylons away to our right are those of the Victoria ground, home of Stoke City Football Club.

Soon the line forks into two and, as the electrified lines disappear away to the right to Stone, Stafford and London, we arrive at the long, empty platforms of **Longton** Station: empty that is apart from one small bus shelter on each platform for the 'comfort' of rail passengers! Soon we go through Meir tunnel and a mile or two further on come to **Blythe Bridge** Station, railhead for the Foxfield Light Railway whose own station is half a mile away in Caverswall Road, and whose line runs for two and a half miles to Foxfield from which it gets its name. Our line heads back into open country passing over a number of level-crossings and passing a number of old fashioned signal-boxes.

After eleven miles of such pleasant scenery, we come to the small town of **Uttoxeter** on the eastern edge of Staffordshire. The market place was once the scene of a somewhat bizzare incident. Dr Johnson's father had owned a bookstall in the market there and his later-to-become-famous son once refused to help his father on the stall, a decision Dr Johnson later bitterly regretted. When Dr Johnson was 70 years of age, he stood in pouring rain on the spot in Uttoxeter

Saddle tank locomotive *Henry Cort*, built in 1903 at Foxfield Colliery on the Foxfield Railway. (*Photo*: Tom Heavyside)

Market Place where his father's bookstall had once stood, in penance for his youthful intractability. In common with most local stations on the line, Uttoxeter's only comfort for rail travellers is a couple of bus shelters. However Uttoxeter's bus shelters are among the smartest on BR, in two-tone blue paint.

As we leave Uttoxeter, we see on the right the racecourse for which Uttoxeter is best known these days, and shortly pass the long-since-closed Marchington Station whose platforms are still *in situ*. Soon after we pass Sudbury level crossing and cross from Staffordshire into Derbyshire. After the next level crossing as Scropton is passed, we see the ruined Tutbury Castle on a hillside to our right. Although we are in Derbyshire, the castle is in Staffordshire, as the River Dove which forms the county boundary at this location runs in between. Tutbury Castle was originally built by the de Ferrers family, but after various forfeitures and restorations it passed to the Crown and was bestowed on John of Gaunt, Duke of Lancaster and fourth son of Edward III, in 1361. It remains the property of the Duchy of Lancaster today. It was ruined in 1646 after its capture by the Roundheads. Mary, Queen of Scots, was imprisoned there three or four times between 1569 and 1585, and both James I and Charles I used the castle as a hunting lodge for the nearby Needwood forest. Tutbury, whose station was closed by the late Dr Beeching, now has a new station, **Tutbury & Hatton**, opened in April 1989. We head back into open country and soon pass Eggington Junction where British Rail's main test track diverges to the left.

Soon lines are sweeping in to join us from the right, coming from Birmingham and Burton-on-Trent. We pass Willington Power Station on our right before a freight-only line goes off to the right at Stenson Junction to run direct to Trent Junction halfway between Derby and Nottingham. We cross the Trent & Mersey Canal once more before the single line from Sinfin comes in from the right as we speed through a derelict-looking **Peartree** Station. The imposing Derby County football ground is then on our left, where only football is played, despite its name of the Baseball Ground. With extensive carriage sidings on our right, we enter **Derby** Station and reach journey's end. Derby Station's frontage has completely changed in the last few years. The City of Derby is well known not only for its importance to rail transport but to road as well with the Rolls Royce factory established in the city in 1907. Derby Cathedral has the second tallest medieval tower in England, Boston stump in Lincolnshire being the tallest. For more information on the city, please see our companion volume *Five Shires by Rail*.

MANCHESTER–BUXTON

by Felix Schmid

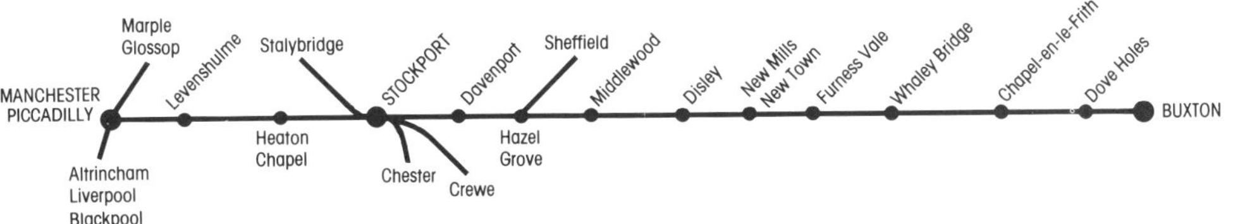

We leave **Manchester Piccadilly** on the tracks of the main line to London Euston. Electrified in 1966, the line was built by the Grand Junction Railway in 1842 and soon taken over by the London & North Western Railway. It runs on an elevated structure past housing estates with frontier names, such as Ford Ardwick, and a history of inadequate design and insufficient maintenance.

Since May 1989 there has been a half-hourly service of 'Sprinter' trains from Manchester to Buxton, with a more frequent service at peak periods. Our journey takes us through the industrial areas of Ardwick and Longsight. At Slade Lane Junction the local line to Styal and Wilmslow forks off to the right. The train stops at **Levenshulme** Station (3 miles), still above street level and situated in a pleasant suburban area with gardens and parks.

After the large McVitie's plant and station at **Heaton Chapel** and the imposing goods warehouse of the LNWR, on the left, we suddenly find ourselves on the huge, four track Stockport Viaduct, one arch of which bridges the River Mersey. Below us on the left, just to the north of the motorway, we should look out for the old railway tunnel, blasted into solid rock, all that remains at this point of the closed line from Godley Junction to Glazebrook. The construction of the brick viaduct was considered a visual disaster in a vale ironically populated by rather ugly cotton mills; it afforded the good citizens of Stockport a unique privilege: in exchange for the permission to build the viaduct they gained, in perpetuity, a mandatory stop for every train using the structure. **Stockport** (population 136,000) has prospered as a result of this decision – many first class passengers board the fast express trains under the splendid stone and iron work of the station (6 miles).

A short distance after Stockport (or Edgeley Station as older railway personnel prefer to call it) we pass the local football ground, leave the main line and enter

A Manchester–Buxton train entering Furness Vale Station. This service is now operated by 'Sprinter' units. (*Photo*: Tom Heavyside)

a deep cutting. We call at **Davenport** ($6\frac{1}{2}$ miles) and reach **Hazel Grove** ($8\frac{1}{2}$ miles), the end of the electrified section of the line. A short distance beyond the station there is a junction where Sheffield-bound trains leave the Buxton line to join the old Midland Railway track leading to New Mills South Junction. The line now rises on to an embankment from which we get a view of part of the Cheshire plain – and lots of bungalow estates. As the Buxton line climbs more steeply and follows Norbury Brook our surroundings start to become rural. Just before the halt at **Middlewood** Station ($10\frac{1}{2}$ miles) we pass under the old railway line from Marple (Rose Hill) to Macclesfield which has been turned into a landscaped footpath and bridleway. After the briefest of stops, in a romantic valley, we may catch a glimpse of the aqueduct carrying the Macclesfield Canal over the railway line. Built to link Manchester and the Potteries this canal is part of the 'Cheshire Ring' and a favourite haunt for canal boat buffs as well as tow path walkers.

The railway line keeps rising, skirts Lyme Park – a paradise for day trippers from the city complete with architectural 'folly' and deer park – and approaches **Disley** (12 miles). Several good pubs and eating places can be found in this refined little town which is also a main access point for the Peak District National Park. This huge nature reserve covers areas of Derbyshire, Cheshire and South Yorkshire and its terrain ranges from pleasant parkland to the barren scenery of the peat bogs. Through a short tunnel we reach the Goyt Valley where we speed, on the level and with only a few yards separating railway and Peak Forest Canal, to **New Mills Newtown** ($13\frac{1}{2}$ miles). Here we are but half a mile from the Midland line to Sheffield, on the other side of the gorge. Still on the level we carry on to **Furness Vale** where The Crossings pub can be recommended for its railway atmosphere.

The next station is **Whaley Bridge**, a strange little industrial town at the upper end of the Peak Forest Canal. This was at one time the trans-shipment point between the canal and the Cromford & High Peak Railway which used a number of steep inclines (a kind of funicular railway) to conquer the Peaks, carrying goods to High Peak Junction south of Matlock on the Cromford Canal. The first of the rope-worked inclines crossed our line from the left just beyond Whaley Bridge station. This peculiar railway was closed in 1967 having been worked to the last by tiny little steam trains.

The River Goyt's upper reaches are to be discovered in a beautiful vale with reservoirs, forests, an old hall in ruins and, at its head, the Cat and Fiddle Inn, one of the highest public houses in England (access by bus from Buxton and Macclesfield on summer Tuesdays, Thursdays and weekends). The train rises past the entrance to this vale and after a short climb we overlook Combs reservoir on the left and get a good view, on the right, of Combs village with its small number of houses and inn.

Our next stop, **Chapel-en-le-Frith** (20 miles), is the starting point for a number of walks which can be exhilarating and, in winter, dangerous. The station is about a mile's walk from the town famous for the huge Ferodo works producing a world supply of brake linings. Continuing our train journey we accelerate onto a viaduct and cross the old Midland Railway line which once ran from London to Manchester via Derby and Matlock. This portion of the old line, Dove Holes Tunnel and Great Rocks Dale to Wye Dale, is still open to ICI's mineral trains originating in the quarries which slowly eat away large chunks of countryside.

After the viaduct and two short tunnels, the LNWR line turns to travel almost due south, briefly pauses at **Dove Holes** ($22\frac{1}{2}$ miles, four houses and an inn) and, after a mile's climb, reaches the highest point of the line, Bibbington Summit at almost 1200 feet. This stretch is famed for snow-drifts in winter and occasionally the A6 road is blocked. Buxton would be left isolated without the railway. The train gathers speed for the remaining two miles to **Buxton** ($25\frac{1}{2}$ miles) where we come to a halt about an hour after leaving Manchester. The resort's railway station is remarkable for its architecture (Sir Joseph Paxton, architect of the Crystal Palace was responsible for its design, note the end wall with its rosette) and for the remaining traces of its earlier duality: the LNWR buildings used to be but one half of the station, the mirror image owned by the Midland Railway, both buildings originally splendidly covered in glass.

Today PeakRail owns the site of the demolished Midland half of the station. Its members have transformed a shed into a museum and run steam trains on weekends. The ultimate goal of the society is the rebuilding and operation of the old line as far as Matlock. This railway will lead through some of Britain's most beautiful and wild scenery: Wye Dale, Chee Dale, Millers Dale, Monsal Dale and Darley Dale, evocative names all. The town of Bakewell will be just one of the attractions of the line whose rebuilding will take some time to be completed. For more details on Buxton see page 56.

PEAKRAIL

by John Snell, Chairman, PeakRail plc

PeakRail was formed in the mid-1970s with the aim of reconstructing and operating the closed section of the Midland Railway's Derby–Manchester route between Matlock and Buxton. The organisation originally comprised an enthusiast society, the Peak Railway Society, and an operating company, Peak Rail (Operations) Ltd. These have now been amalgamated to form PeakRail plc.

PeakRail plc owns the three-acre Buxton Midland Station site where a thriving steam centre has been established. The company also leases land and buildings from BR and West Derbyshire District Council at Matlock Station, where a shop, café and loco restoration building have been developed, and from West Derbyshire District Council at Darley Dale where the up side station building and platform have been renovated. The station building is now a hostel for PeakRail volunteers and ramblers. A recent development is the opening of a Red Star parcels agency at Matlock Station.

From 1979 a number of attempts were made to obtain planning permission for the whole twenty-mile route, but on each occasion these were rejected on highway safety grounds, the highway authorities fearing that road access and parking provision would be inadequate for the scale of project envisaged. However, early in 1986, West Derbyshire District Council did give planning permission on a five-year basis for the Matlock–Darley Dale section and outline planning permission has now been granted for the whole Matlock–Buxton route. Four hundred yards of track has now been laid at Darley Dale and a second steam centre is being established there. Attention is currently being concentrated on reopening the Matlock to Darley Dale section.

In 1979–81, PeakRail operated a charter public Sunday service on the Derby–Matlock line. This demonstrated the viability of the service and in 1982 it was taken over on a revenue support basis by Derbyshire County Council. From 1983 to date it has been wholly operated by BR, without any revenue support.

The section of the Matlock–Buxton line between Buxton and Blackwell Mill ($3\frac{3}{4}$ miles) is still operated by BR as a freight line to service the extensive quarries between Blackwell Mill and Chinley. In 1985, PeakRail operated a profit-sharing DMU service with BR over this line as part of a Buxton–New Mills Central public service (Sundays only), making connections with Hope Valley trains. The service, called 'The Peak Rail Rambler', was extremely successful and did not need to call on the revenue guarantee offered by Derbyshire County Council. The service ran again in 1986, this time as a PeakRail charter, three trains running on every Sunday in July and August, the first two Sundays in September and August Bank Holiday Monday. The middle train of the three was routed via the Hazel Grove Chord. Agreement was reached with BR to construct a halt at Blackwell Mill for the 1987 season and this opened under the name of Chee Dale halt. The service did not operate in 1988 following insistence by the Railway Inspectorate that certain signalling improvements were necessary for the regular operation of passenger trains over the Chinley–Buxton line. PeakRail have now agreed to fund these improvements and it is hoped that the 'Rambler' will again operate in 1990, running from Buxton to Edale via the Chinley East Chord.

At Buxton, a grant of £30,000 was received from the former Greater Manchester Council to assist in replacing the missing bridge which separates Buxton Midland Station from the Ashwood Dale line. This project is scheduled for completion in Spring 1989 and, following completion of a junction agreement with BR, the 'Rambler' service then will be able to operate from Midland Station for the 1990 and subsequent seasons. The long-term intention is to re-lay a second track alongside the BR line between Buxton and Blackwell Mill.

MANCHESTER–STOCKPORT/ STYAL–CREWE

by Felix Schmid

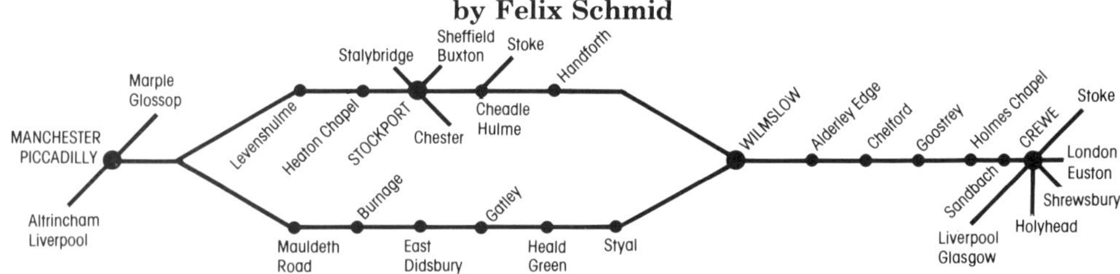

The local service from Manchester to Crewe via Stockport is basically hourly and is operated by class 303 and 304 electric units. In addition there are two-hourly 'Sprinter Express' services to Cardiff calling only at Stockport and Wilmslow and InterCity services to London Euston and Birmingham, again calling only at Stockport and (some) at Wilmslow. We leave **Manchester Piccadilly** and follow the route of the Buxton trains as far as **Stockport**. The twenty-seven-arch Stockport Viaduct, Europe's largest brick structure, which is 110 feet high and contains eleven million bricks, is currently being cleaned under a project sponsored by the Manpower Services Commission. When this is complete the viaduct will be spectacularly floodlit at night, which should make a fine sight. At Edgeley Junction our line continues straight on after the Buxton line has disappeared to the left. To the right is the line to Chester via Altrincham, reopened to passengers in May 1989.

The Macclesfield line leaves to our left at **Cheadle Hulme**, a V-shaped station with an LNW signal-box on the right-hand side. After traversing some open country the train calls at **Handforth** Station and crosses the River Dean. The old hall of the Breretons in Handforth dates from 1562. The Styal line approaches from the right and both lines cross the River Bollin on separate viaducts. They join at **Wilmslow** Station, which is served by InterCity services to the south. Wilmslow (population 30,000) is a prosperous town, the first in Britain to have its own credit card, valid only in Wilmslow shops. Only a short stretch of farmland separates Wilmslow from **Alderley Edge**, a residential area. The town owes its name to a dramatic sandstone escarpment 650 feet high and two miles long which

Manchester Oxford Road–Alderley Edge train in sylvan surroundings arriving at Styal Station in May 1985. (*Photo*: Tom Heavyside)

is owned by the National Trust and which offers a commanding viewpoint towards the Cheshire Plain and the hills of North Wales. The Edge is at its best on an autumn evening. A sunset on Alderley Edge is a very special experience, and well worth the effort!

The area south of Alderley Edge is still relatively unspoilt. Meandering lanes, hedges, streams, beautiful old farmhouses and lovingly-restored farm labourers' cottages characterise the landscape. Woods, copses and small valleys alternate with large open expanses, with hamlets here and there. The railway line passes Nether Alderley, on the left, and reaches **Chelford**, the 'hub' of many cycle events. Chelford Station serves a small community and a large cattle market regularly takes place adjacent to the station. South of Chelford there are loop lines on either side of the main line. On our left the colossal radio telescope of Jodrell Bank, which is open to the public, towers above the lanes before **Goostrey** Station. The 250-foot dish of the 1957 Mark I telescope is fully steerable and supported by two 180-foot metal towers. The Mark II telescope alongside is a 125-foot elliptic paraboloid. There is a large exhibition hall on the site and an excellent planetarium. Goostrey village (turn right outside the station) is quaint and compact with a church and two pubs.

Our train now crosses a 1,794-foot-long, twenty-three-arch brick viaduct over the River Dane before **Holmes Chapel** Station. Turn right at the main road and right at the traffic lights for the town with its fine medieval church. The line from here is straight and on the flat and there is only a short cutting just before reaching **Sandbach** Station. The station is actually situated in Elworth, Sandbach being a mile to the east. Here the freight and diversionary route from Northwich joins the main line from the right. Sandbach has several half-timbered buildings and a pair of ancient stone crosses in the town centre. The seventh-century crosses, which were pieced together in 1816, are supposed to represent the conversion and marriage of Peada, son of King Penda.

The four-track section from Sandbach to Crewe has suffered badly from salt subsidence over the years but has now stabilised. Note the lakes on either side of the line with their half-submerged trees. These were caused by brine pumping and are known as 'flashes'. We now enter the northern outskirts of **Crewe** and at Sydney Bridge Junction the independent lines, used by freight trains to avoid Crewe Station, dive down to our right and we curve round to the left to arrive at journey's end at one of British Rail's key junction stations.

CHELFORD–GOOSTREY
A Taste of Cycling in the Cheshire Lanes
Out of the station turn right onto the A537, turn left into the next country lane towards Peover Superior. Go straight on at a number of T-junctions and at a crossroads. Turn left at the second crossroads, then right at the second T-junction, straight across the next crossroads and through the railway underpass. Do not miss the view of the old mill, the viaduct and the stream before your climb to the T-junction. Turn right, cycle over the railway line and turn left at Bellmarsh House. Follow the railway line into Goostrey, and turn left to reach the station.

THE STYAL LINE
In the great plan of things the electrified suburban railway line from **Manchester Piccadilly** to Wilmslow via Styal does not seem to figure very prominently. The line, built by the London & North Western Railway in 1909, has a half-hourly local service off peak, and in 1989 there will be trains on Sundays in the summer only as an experiment by Greater Manchester Passenger Transport Executive. Outward appearances can be misleading though; the line has in fact several important assets. Apart from its function as a relief route for freight traffic bypassing Stockport it serves one of the most important industrial museums in Britain, situated in an outstanding country park. Close by is Manchester Airport which will hopefully be connected to the Styal line in May 1993.

Our train leaves Piccadilly on its southern side, across from the former Mayfield station. We travel on the main Crewe line as far as Slade Lane Junction where we veer off to the right. We enter a long stretch of absolutely straight track, high up on an embankment. Shortly before reaching our first stop at **Mauldeth Road**, we cross the closed Fallowfield loop freight line. Travelling high above the roofs of the semi-detached houses we are offered views into back gardens and down onto parks. Somewhat more scenic though is the back-drop to the east: the blue contours of the peaks in the shimmering haze of a hot summer's day offer a memorable spectacle. In winter it's snow-covered hills, sharply defined against a blue sky, which add a bit of romantic flavour to the journey to work.

The train calls at **Burnage** and crosses the track-bed of the old Midland line from Derby to Manchester near to the point where the proposed Greater Manchester light rail system may one day have a southern terminus. In between the stops at **East Didsbury** and **Gatley** the line bridges the River Mersey and somehow manages to find its way through the junction of the M56 and M63. We also cross the single freight line from Northenden to New Mills and the recently-reopened Northenden to Stockport line. South of Gatley the line continues in a cutting; the airport, on our right just after **Heald Green** Station, is therefore not visible. The last call is at **Styal** (see below) and a viaduct then carries the train across the River Dean. We cross the River Bollin, a tributary of the Mersey, and reach **Wilmslow** station, $11\frac{1}{2}$ miles from Manchester.

WILMSLOW–STYAL
A Walk into the Industrial Past
Turn right out of Wilmslow station and cross the A34 at the traffic lights. Walk more or less due west for 500 yards on a residential street until you can cross 'The Carrs' on a footpath. Walk north-west to a footbridge across the River Bollin. Use the B5166 to cross the River Dean. Turn left immediately onto a footpath which enters the National Trust property. Follow the enchanting wooded vale of the River Bollin, past the reconstructed mill pond, to the large, but well-proportioned, buildings of Quarry Bank Mill. In 1784 Samuel Greg from Belfast built his cotton mill in this remote valley, chosen for its abundant water supply. The mill was closed in 1959 having used power from a water turbine to the last. A giant water

wheel was again installed in the mill in 1984/5 and it now drives some of the looms in the working museum. There are demonstrations of the entire process from waterwheel to woven cloth, and a new gallery explains the process of textile finishing, including bleaching, dyeing and printing. The mill is open daily from June to September from 11 a.m. to 5 p.m. and daily except Monday from October to May from 11 a.m. to 4 p.m. (5 p.m. in April and May). Styal Country Park is open daily from dawn to dusk. Continue the walk through the picturesque and well-preserved Styal Village, built by the Gregs. It is one of the earliest factory colonies complete with Apprentice House, school, general store and chapel. Styal Station is nearby, to the north-east, approximately one hour of walking.

CHEADLE HULME–KIDSGROVE

by Basil Jeuda

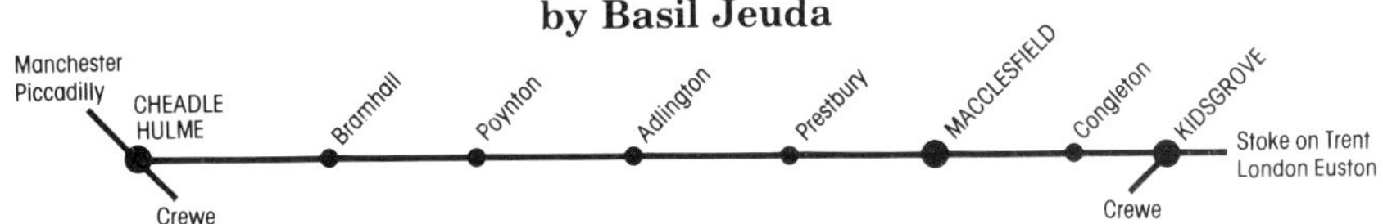

The line from Cheadle Hulme to Kidsgrove was basically constructed in two parts. The first section was commissioned by the former Manchester & Birmingham Railway (later to become the London & North Western Railway) and was opened in 1845 as far as Beech Lane in Macclesfield. The stretch from Beech Lane, Macclesfield to Stoke-on-Trent was opened in July 1849, and was constructed by the former North Staffordshire Railway Company (NSR).

The **Cheadle Hulme** station was modernised as part of the electrification programme in the late 1950s and early 1960s, but the London & North Western Railway signal-box survives at the junction. The local service to Kidsgrove is provided by class 303 or 304 electric units and is basically hourly, running through to Stoke.

The next station that we come to is **Bramhall** which is an important commuter station in the area. The recently-renovated half-timbered Bramall Hall, an outstanding example of the black and white Tudor style, is ¾ mile north of the station (turn right at the main road). The oldest parts of the hall were built in 1375 when the estate came to John de Davenport through his marriage into the local de Bromale family. His coat-of-arms can be seen in the fifteenth-century stained glass. The greatest treasure in the hall is a heraldic table carpet made around 1565 which bears a Tudor shield and is twenty feet long. There are also some unique wall paintings dating from the sixteenth and early seventeenth centuries, which have recently been restored. The 100 acres of parkland were landscaped by the Victorian Charles Nevill in the style of Capability Brown. There is a nature trail and formal garden. The hall is open daily except Mondays and the whole of January (except New Year's Day), Christmas Day and Boxing Day, from April to September from 10 a.m. to 5 p.m. and from October to March from 1 p.m. to 4 p.m. The free guided tour leaves at 2.15 p.m.

A mile or so beyond Bramhall, we come to the disused sidings of an oil distribution company on the right-hand side. About a mile beyond that we approach Poynton Station, and to the left can be seen the track bed of the former mineral railway that went towards the main Hazel Grove/Macclesfield road and across the road up to the Poynton collieries by way of an incline system. The Poynton collieries closed in the summer of 1935. On the right-hand side of the station can be seen through the trees a garment factory which is housed in the former London & North Western Railway goods shed. The station at **Poynton** was opened in 1887 and replaced an earlier station called Midway half a mile or so towards Macclesfield. Poynton Station is very well preserved and is beautifully maintained in the colours of the former London Midland & Scottish Railway Company, of which the line was a part from 1923 to 1948.

Leaving Poynton, you will pass the former Midway Station, which is at the head of a terrace of old properties half a mile or so on the left. This station was opened in 1845 and closed in 1887, and is to the design of the Manchester & Birmingham Railway. The next station that is reached is **Adlington**, which is of a completely different design, more in line with the design features of Stockport Station. On leaving Adlington the line crosses the main Hazel Grove/Macclesfield road and then enters into a deep cutting which shortly becomes Prestbury Tunnel. As you leave the tunnel, you enter **Prestbury** Station (7 miles from Cheadle Hulme) with the station building on the right-hand side being the only Manchester & Birmingham Railway station building still in operational use as a station. Notice the attractive waiting-rooms of a rather unusual design on either side of the station. Turn left at the main road for the picturesque Prestbury village with several half-timbered buildings.

The line between Prestbury and Macclesfield, a former silk town, follows the course of the River Bollin which you will see on the right-hand side, and after two miles or so you enter Macclesfield Tunnel, on leaving which you pass through the site of the former Macclesfield Hibel Road Station. As you enter **Macclesfield** Station (the former Macclesfield Central Station) you will see on the left-hand side the highly ornate and Italian-designed building of Arighi Bianchi, the house furnishers, whilst on the right-hand side, overlooking the market place, is Macclesfield parish church. The new Silk Museum, housed in an early nineteenth-century Sunday school, won the prestigious 'Come to Britain' trophy in 1988 and the West Park Museum in Prestbury Road has an interesting collection of Egyptology. Macclesfield Station was modernised in 1960 in advance of electrification. It is served by InterCity as well as local services. The station itself straddles the River Bollin and trailing in from the left-hand side can just be seen the track-bed left of the former Macclesfield, Bollington & Marple Railway.

On leaving the station, the River Bollin is visible on the right-hand side. The railway line snakes through the centre of the industrial area of Macclesfield and then starts a 1 in 112 climb towards the Peat Moss on the edge of the town. There was a moss peat factory on the site from a period from the early 1890s to 1965. On the left-hand side can be seen the Macclesfield Canal which crosses the railway twice between Macclesfield and Congleton.

After about four miles, the village of North Rode is reached in a cutting and to the left veers off the track bed of the scenic Churnet Valley line to Leek and Uttoxeter which closed for regular passenger traffic in 1960. We now cross the NSR Dane Viaduct which is 1,275 feet long, with twenty arches, each with a span of fifty feet. Two miles or so further on we again cross over a viaduct and underneath can be seen the track-bed of the former NSR Biddulph Valley Railway line connecting Congleton on the right with Biddulph and Stoke-on-Trent.

Congleton Station (17¾ miles from Cheadle Hulme), is shortly reached and on the right-hand side can be seen two different types of railway cottages and the former NSR goods shed. This is a modern station but on the left-hand side as we cross the canal can be seen the old station-master's house, made of cream coloured brick. Congleton, traditionally a yarn manufacturing town, has three old inns and a town hall containing a collection of interesting relics. In the adjoining village of Havanna, cigars were once made. The town has a fine parish church dating from 1742, which retains its galleries and box-pews. Four miles south-west of Congleton is Little Moreton Hall dating from 1589 and a perfect example of black and white domestic architecture.

Leaving Congleton, in about a mile and half, we pass the village of Astbury, and in particular on the left-hand side can be seen the lime kilns, now disused, for firing the lime which came from the only limestone outcrop in Cheshire. A mile beyond we reach the area of Mow Cop, and on the right-hand side can be seen the station-master's house and we shortly pass the NSR Mow Cop signal-box. On the left-hand side is the imposing Mow Cop, an eighteenth-century folly. We shortly reach the site of the original Kidsgrove Station, which was the start of the famous Loop Line linking the pottery towns of Tunstall, Burslem, Hanley, Etruria and Stoke-on-Trent. We then enter the present **Kidsgrove** Station (23¼ miles from Cheadle Hulme) an important junction, with the line from Crewe coming in on the right-hand side. The original NSR footbridge can be seen at the end of the platforms.

MANCHESTER–BREDBURY/ HYDE–NEW MILLS

by Felix Schmid

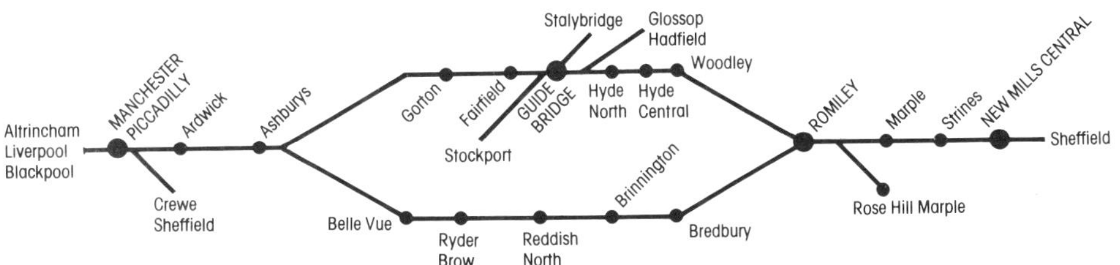

Today there exist two rail routes between Manchester and Marple's two stations. The trains to Rose Hill, operating at hourly intervals during the day, mostly travel via Bredbury. Those to Marple and New Mills, also hourly, alternate between this line and the 'Hyde Loop'. There is an hourly through service to Sheffield via Hyde Central and New Mills.

MANCHESTER–ROSE HILL MARPLE via BREDBURY

We depart from one of the low-numbered platforms at Piccadilly and leave the London line at **Ardwick** Station. On our left are the remains of the vast sidings which once served the enormous freight traffic over the Woodhead route. After calling at **Ashburys** we leave this route, cross under the A57 and stop at the resited **Belle Vue** Station which serves the industrial and housing estates that have taken over from the famous zoo. The line from Ashburys to New Mills was formerly jointly owned by the Midland and Great Central Railways. The next calling point, **Ryder Brow**, is a new station financed by the former Greater Manchester Council, sited close to the bridge which carries the closed goods line from Gorton to Trafford Park over our line, formerly electrified as far as Reddish depot and in 1987 used to demonstrate a light rail vehicle at Debdale Park.

The Stockport Canal once crossed the railway on an aqueduct, before **Reddish North** Station. On leaving Reddish, we pass under the Stockport–Stalybridge line and suddenly emerge onto Reddish Vale Viaduct, said to be one of England's most beautiful, overlooking the wide expanse of the Tame Valley. The river meanders through a green plain with reservoirs and backwaters. We may spot the odd angler and certainly some water birds. We pass the former Reddish Junction which once linked our line with Stockport (Tiviot Dale) and call at **Brinnington**, a station opened by Greater Manchester Passenger Transport

27

'Pacer' train in the livery of Greater Manchester Passenger Transport Executive leaving Manchester Piccadilly for New Mills Central. (*Photo*: Tom Heavyside)

Executive. We cross over a stone terminal situated on the former Godley to Glazebrook line before **Bredbury**, one of Stockport's suburbs which extends to our right. After two short tunnels, we may catch a glimpse on the left of the idyllic setting in which the Peak Forest Canal follows the railway. **Romiley** Station, not far from the old established works of Davies & Metcalfe, suppliers of air brake equipment, is an example of a reasonably well-preserved older station. It overlooks the main street and church (see below for a suggested walk). After a cutting the *pièce de résistance*: the railway line crosses the River Goyt on a high arched stone viaduct of very pleasing proportions. Alongside it runs the Peak Forest Canal on its equally impressive aqueduct, complete with towpath. Immediately after the viaduct the **Rose Hill** branch leaves the main line at Marple Wharf Junction. The train stops after less than a mile: this is all that is left of the railway line which once followed the contours to Macclesfield. Its track-bed forms a path offering splendid views across the Cheshire plain.

MANCHESTER–HYDE–MARPLE and NEW MILLS

Trains to New Mills via Hyde use the same route as the Glossop trains as far as Hyde Junction, west of **Hyde North** Station. The line to Romiley turns south at this point and crosses the M67 motorway before **Hyde Central** Station. The Peak Forest Canal and the River Tame are both on our right. On a nice day it is well worth walking the approximately three miles from Hyde to Romiley along the bank of the canal.

The freight line from Godley formerly joined from the left at Apethorne Junction. We arrive at **Woodley**, a junction where the Cheshire Lines Railway left for Glazebrook. After a few hundred yards on an embankment we join the Bredbury line just before calling at **Romiley**. The Goyt valley viaduct brings us to the modern station of **Marple**, a picturesque country town. The Peak Forest Canal's flight of locks crosses the railway just before the station. Following and re-crossing the River Goyt we reach **Strines**, an unstaffed halt. The views from the train along this stretch of the line are beautiful. On the one side the river valley with Marple Ridge and Disley as a backdrop, on the other side the hills, the start of the Peak District. Soon we reach **New Mills Central** with its old, well-kept station where ramblers once changed for the now vanished Hayfield line. From New Mills the line continues through two short tunnels to join the main Manchester–Sheffield line at New Mills South Junction.

A Walk through Transport History
A very worthwhile ramble takes us from Romiley Station down the small lane which starts just opposite the station; we continue past a church, negotiate the underpass, and scale the steps to the canal towpath. With the canal on our left we head through open countryside near Oakwood Hall and suddenly find ourselves above the River Goyt on an aqueduct. We cross the canal at the foot of an impressive flight of sixteen locks which raise the level of the canal by about 275 feet. Perhaps a bit out of breath from assisting the boat travellers with the arduous task of operating the locks we reach the top opposite the lock-keepers' cottages. We now have a number of choices: we may like to call into one of the local hostelries, join a party for a canal boat trip, follow the Peak Forest Canal to Whaley Bridge and Buxworth (7 miles, about two hours) or continue along the Macclesfield Canal. The fourth option takes us along the towpath through fields for about two miles (three-quarters of an hour). Shortly after crossing the A6 look down on the Buxton line from the aqueduct carrying the canal. Two hundred yards further on we descend from the bank via a small lane. After Pool House Farm we turn right and join the Middlewood way which brings us to the station of the same name.

SHEFFIELD–MANCHESTER PICCADILLY VIA THE HOPE VALLEY
by Tim Young and Denis Bradbury

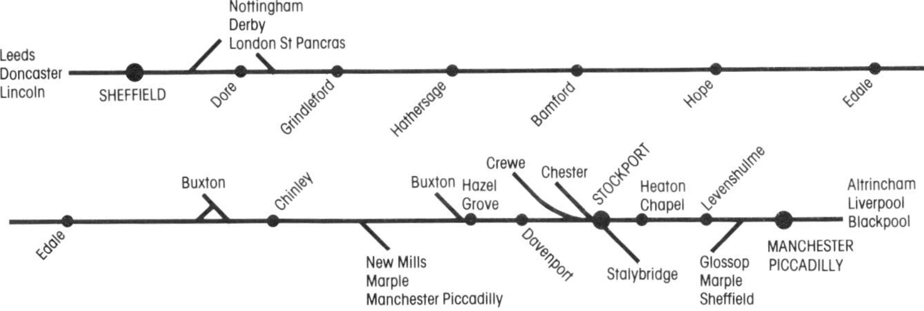

Our train may well have started its journey at Norwich, Ipswich, Cambridge or Harwich, although hourly local trains also operate between Sheffield and Manchester via the Hope Valley and Romiley, calling at all stations between Sheffield and New Mills. The route through the Hope Valley was opened by the Midland Railway in 1893, nearly fifty years after the more northerly Woodhead route, which had opened in 1845. As we commence our journey through the hilly southern suburbs of **Sheffield**, the valley through which we're passing is that of the River Sheaf, from which the city gets its name.

After about four miles of climbing a 1 in 100 gradient we diverge from the main line to London St Pancras and pass the Abbeydale Industrial Hamlet on the right-hand side. This unique eighteenth-century works is the only surviving relic of the original cutlery industry of Sheffield, which was situated in the Sheaf Valley. The hamlet, which is open throughout the year except on Christmas Day, contains crucible melting furnaces, water-driven forges, grinding shops and blacksmith's shops, cottages and warehouses. The mill dam at the side of the line provides the water power for the wheels. Not far away are the remains of Beauchief Abbey, founded in 1175; only the western tower remains, but it is still used for church services on Sundays.

Just before reaching the first local station at **Dore**, the train crosses the River Limb as it flows into the Sheaf. The river formerly marked the boundary between the Saxon kingdoms of Northumbria and Wessex and it was also a county and diocesan boundary. Dore Station, formerly Dore & Totley, has been reduced to a single platform on the Hope Valley line only but is still well-patronized by the locals. The station was built following an agreement between the Duke of Devonshire, who owned most of the surrounding land, and the Midland Railway. A mile away up the hill to the right of the line is the village of Dore. In the year 827, a treaty was signed here between Egbert, king of Wessex, and Eanred, king of Northumbria, which made Egbert king of the whole English-speaking race from the Firth of Forth to the English Channel, and thus brought about the union of England.

Immediately after Dore we curve away to the right whilst the main line to Chesterfield and beyond disappears away to the left. You will then notice on the left a single line curving in to join us. This line enables trains to run direct between Chesterfield and Manchester without the need to reverse in Sheffield. Some of the new services recently introduced, especially certain key trains used by businessmen, use this curve to reduce journey times between the East Midlands and Manchester.

About a mile further on we pass Totley Tunnel East signal-box to our left and enter the murky depths of Totley Tunnel, 3 miles 950 yards long and the second longest rail tunnel in Britain, only the Severn Tunnel being longer. It took four years to build the tunnel, the navvies working on it having to contend with vast quantities of water. At one time during the construction, 26,000 gallons of water were being pumped out every hour. It was said that every navvy working in the tunnel was like Moses – whenever he struck the rock, water gushed out. Water is still a considerable problem in the tunnel today, involving British Rail in a good deal of maintenance. By contrast the Woodhead route had a nearly-new tunnel, opened as recently as 1954, which was dry and lit by electricity throughout its length.

Apart from the water troubles, the major landowners under whose land the tunnel was driven had to be placated. The Duke of Rutland claimed that the tunnel would interfere with his grouse-shooting on the moors above and all work in the tunnel was suspended between August 12th and October 1st – the shooting

Nottingham–Blackpool train coming off the Hazel Grove Chord line in May 1987. This service is now operated by 'Super Sprinter' units. (*Photo*: Tom Heavyside)

season. Inside the tunnel we pass from British Rail's Eastern Region to the London Midland Region.

On emerging from the tunnel we immediately enter **Grindleford** Station in the Derwent Valley. Grindleford is a typical and pleasant little Derbyshire village in the heart of the Peak District and there are beautiful walks along the Derwent both north and south of the village. Grindleford is also a good railhead for anyone wanting to walk in the hills and the Leam Hall youth hostel is three-quarters of a mile north of the village. To the north are the Longshaw moors and to the north west where the A625 climbs Millstone Edge is the great panorama known as The Surprise. Above the village, millstones were cut out of the living rock and sold all over the country to grind grain. Unfinished stones can still be found in various quarries. On the right-hand side near the station is Padley Chapel – a stone building used for many years as a cattle shed. The chapel belonged to Padley Hall, the seat of the Eyre family who were staunch Catholics. In 1588, during a search, two Catholic priests were found hiding in the hall. They were taken to Derby and hanged, drawn and quartered for the crime of being priests and thus traitors to Queen Elizabeth I. John Fitzherbert, who was living in the hall at the time, was also put to death and the estates confiscated.

From Grindleford the line turns northwards alongside the River Derwent to **Hathersage** – a pleasant little town which is mentioned in Charlotte Brontë's *Jane Eyre* under the pseudonym of Morton. Charlotte Brontë stayed in Hathersage in 1852 and took the name of her character from the prominent Derbyshire family. The west tower of St Michael's Church dates from the fourteenth century and the battlements and font are of fifteenth-century origin. The church contains two chairs made of locally-quarried stone for Queen Victoria and Prince Albert for the opening of St Georges Hall in Liverpool. There is also a very fine set of brasses of the Eyre family, who were lords of the manor from the early fifteenth century. The earliest brass is of Robert Eyre, who fought at the battle of Agincourt and died in 1459, and his wife Jean. The glass in the east window came from Derwent church, now submerged under a reservoir. Robin Hood's friend Little John is said to have been born in Hathersage and to have returned there to die after burying Robin Hood at Kirklees in Yorkshire. His reputed grave is some ten feet long.

We journey on to **Bamford**, where the railway crosses the River Derwent. To the north of Bamford are several reservoirs, the most famous of which is the Ladybower reservoir, whose dam can briefly be seen from the train. The reservoirs supply water to Sheffield, Derby, Nottingham and Leicester. There is a sparse bus service in the summer between Bamford and the Ladybower reservoir. Bamford Church, built in 1860, has an unusual square spire on a narrow square tower. Two miles beyond Bamford is **Hope**, the railhead for Castleton, with which it is connected by a reasonably frequent bus service. The hills surrounding Castleton contain four interesting sets of limestone caves. These comprise the Peak Cavern, Treak Cavern, the Speedwell mine which is visited by a trip in a boat along an underground canal built to drain water from the mine, and higher up on the hillside the Blue John Mine, where the famous Blue John rock is obtained. Above Castleton stands the ruin of Peverill Castle, dating from the time of William the Conqueror and woven into Scott's *Peveril of the Peak*.

The name Hope means 'valley' and so the term 'Hope Valley' is somewhat tautologous. The village is situated near the confluence of the Peakshole Water and the River Noe. The old part of the village is built of gritstone and St Peter's Church is mainly early fourteenth century, including the tower. There is the shaft of a ninth-century Saxon cross in the churchyard. An agricultural show and sheep-dog trials are held on August bank holiday and the well-dressing takes place on the nearest Sunday to St Peter's day (29 June). From Hope Station the line climbs on a steady gradient of 1 in 100 to the summit in Cowburn Tunnel, following the course of the Noe. Soon after leaving Hope, a freight branch runs off to the left on its way to Earles Cement Works on the far side of the valley. The works can be seen in the distance, the 300-foot chimney being one of the tallest in England.

We head on to the head of the valley and come to the next station, **Edale**, which has a Midland Railway signal-box with a curious tall spike at each of its gable ends. Edale is a favourite centre for tourists and hikers and marks the southern end of the Pennine Way, which stretches for some 250 miles along the summit of the Pennines to Kirk Yetholm on the northern slopes of the Cheviots. The correct name of the village is Edale Chapel and the village has an old inn, the Nag's Head, and some gritstone cottages dating from the seventeenth century. Beyond Edale village is Kinder Scout, generally known as The Peak. It is a featureless plateau of heather and peat, several square miles in area, 2,088 feet above sea level at its highest point – no place to be caught in a mist without a compass and map! Here mention may be made of the 'Mass Trespass' by hundreds of people onto Kinder Scout on April 4 1932 in support of the Access to Mountains Bill, which had been regularly rejected by Parliament since it had first been introduced in 1888. The demonstrators were met by a strong force of police and gamekeepers. Five ramblers were arrested and sentenced at Derby Assizes to between two and six months' imprisonment. The Bill finally became law in 1949 and opened the moorlands to the public for the greater part of the year. There are fears that the current water privatisation proposals may again threaten access to the country-side.

The traveller may well wonder why a flat-topped hill should be called The Peak. The name of the Peak District given to this part of the Pennines has nothing to do with the shape of the hills, but derives from Pecsetan, the name of a Celtic tribe who lived in this area in pre-Roman times. Over the centuries, Pecsetan was changed into Peak. A mile from Edale the train enters Cowburn Tunnel, two miles 182 yards long and 875 feet below the moor. It has the distinction of being the deepest tunnel on any British railway.

From the western portal of Cowburn Tunnel the train travels a further three miles to **Chinley**, passing the triangular junction with the former Midland main line to Derby and London St Pancras on the left. This line now goes to Buxton only and is heavily used by stone trains from the extensive quarries in Peak Dale. From 1985 to 1987 this line was used by a summer weekend DMU service in connection with Peak Rail's preservation scheme at Buxton. Normally, would-be rail travellers from Sheffield to the Derbyshire spa town of Buxton must alight at New Mills Central and walk half a mile to New Mills Newtown, which is served by trains on the Manchester–Buxton line.

As the Hope Valley train approaches Chinley Station, one can look back on the right-hand side and see the Cowburn Tunnel ventilator, high up on the moorland skyline. Chinley Station itself, 700 feet above sea level, must rank as one of the coldest in the country on which to wait for a train. Like Dore it was once an important junction station but is now merely a wayside halt. From Chinley the line follows the valleys of the Black Brook and the River Goyt. We descend a 1 in 90 gradient and pass the former Buxworth station to our left. At New Mills South Junction local trains fork right, bridging two gorges and piercing an intervening rock at the approach to **New Mills Central**. Longer-distance 'Sprinter Express' services to Manchester and Liverpool continue straight on over a viaduct to enter the gloom of yet another long tunnel, Disley, two miles 346 yards long. Soon after emerging, passenger trains turn right over the Hazel Grove Chord line to join the Buxton–Manchester line just south of **Hazel Grove** Station. The modest investment by British Rail in building the chord line has sensibly knitted together uncoordinated lines inherited from competing companies and enables Sheffield–Manchester trains to call at Stockport. The Bishop of Chester performed the opening ceremony for the chord in 1986 as part of it was constructed on church-owned land.

We are now in Greater Manchester and from Hazel Grove station there are overhead wires for the local electric trains, although these are now little used with a half-hourly service of 'Sprinter' trains to Buxton. We speed through Davenport Station and curve round to join the Euston–Manchester line at Edgeley Junction no 1, still guarded by a London & North Western Railway signal-box. **Stockport** is our only stop before **Manchester Piccadilly** and we take the fast pair of tracks to reach journey's end at one of the recently-lengthened through platforms 13 and 14. For a more detailed description of the line between Hazel Grove and Manchester, please see the section on the Manchester–Buxton line.

MANCHESTER–GLOSSOP–HADFIELD
by Kathy Sanderson

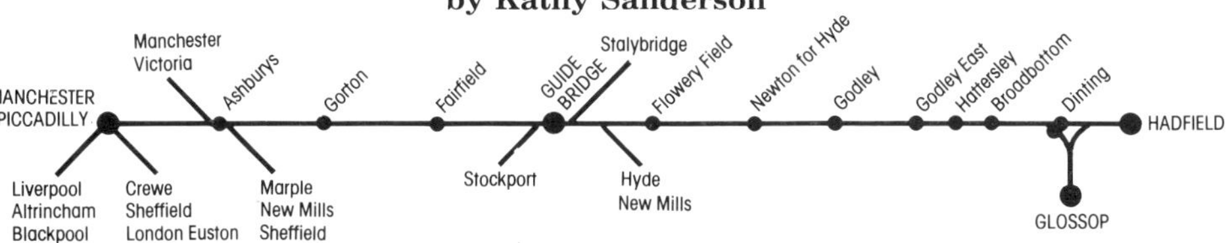

It is no longer possible to travel to Sheffield or London from Manchester via the Great Central main line, but some of the finest scenery in the area is within easy access of Glossop and Hadfield, the present terminus of the electric service from Manchester Piccadilly. There are also many walks and places of interest to visit close to some stations. The basic half-hourly service is augmented to quarter-hourly at peak times. There is a Sunday service from May to October.

The line winds its way through the industrialised area of Ardwick to the first stop at **Ashburys**. The friary church of St Francis, referred to locally as 'The Monastery', is situated on Gorton Lane, close to Ashburys Station. This fine neo-Gothic building dates from 1862 and is home for a community of Franciscan monks. The friary is best visited between 10 a.m. and 10.30 a.m. An aqueduct on the Stockport branch of the Ashton Canal crosses the line just outside **Gorton** Station. The canal has been filled in and serves as a footpath. Outside the station turn right and right again into Brightman Street, right into Longford Street and through a gap in the hedge to gain access to the footpath. **Fairfield** Station was built in anticipation of a plan that never materialised. A racecourse was to be built nearby, and the station had six platforms to cater for the large numbers of passengers anticipated. The idea was abandoned, and the station is now sur-rounded by a large expanse of open land upon which there are several reservoirs.

Fairfield Square, which is within easy reach of Fairfield Station (turn right outside the station, turn left at the main road and right into Fairfield Avenue) is the site of the largest Moravian settlement in England. The Moravians originally came from Czechoslovakia and had previously settled in Saxony and North America. They were driven out of the established Church and began to form 'settlements'. The farm they purchased in Droylsden, which they called Fairfield, is held on a 999-year lease from 15 October 1785. It is built on the 'square within a square' principle, the inner square containing the Chapel, Minister's House and the original Steward's House. The industrious Moravians occupied themselves with a large number of trades including weaving, baking, cotton spinning and

The renovated Broadbottom Station. (*Photo*: James C. Grantham)

hatting and were obviously an asset to the community. W. M. Christy & Sons, the local towel and bedding manufacturers, supplied the settlement with gas in 1837. In 1936 electricity was installed in buildings and streets, and water was supplied from the canal by means of a filter and lead pipes, which were regularly examined. Interestingly, the settlement possessed the only fire engine in Droylsden.

A change of train can be made at **Guide Bridge**, the most important intermediate station on the line, for travel to Stalybridge and onwards to Leeds or York, or to Stockport for the Potteries, Crewe or London. It is also possible to change at Guide Bridge for trains via Hyde to Marple and New Mills. **Flowery Field** Station is one of the new stations financed by Greater Manchester Council and opened in May 1985. **Newton** Station is convenient for the giant Fine Fare hypermarket. Beyond Newton the line passes over the little-used M67 motorway which has proved something of a white elephant. The large Manchester overspill estate at Hattersley was built in 1962/3. **Godley** was the nearest station to the estate until in 1978 the most modern fully-staffed station on the line was opened at **Hattersley**. A new Godley station further west than the previous site opened in 1986, and the former Godley Junction station, now Godley East, is only served by certain peak hour trains.

Broadbottom, the most attractive station on the line, was badly damaged by fire in 1984. The bay window and wooden canopy were completely destroyed, but British Rail reconstructed the booking office and part of the station building. Thornhill Leisure Development have converted the 142-year-old station building into a pub/restaurant, appropriately called The Station. There are separate dining rooms for smokers and non-smokers. The restaurant is open from 12 noon to 2 p.m. and 6 p.m. to 10 p.m. Monday to Saturday and all day Sunday. It is advisable to book a table and the telephone number is 0457-63327. Turn to the right outside the station for a pleasant walk of approximately three miles. Follow the main road through the village and to Charlesworth. In the centre of Charlesworth a left turn into Town Lane leads eventually to Dinting Vale, but at the highest point of the road there are extensive views over the valley, almost as far as Hadfield. The road drops down via Glossop Road to the junction with the A57, the Snake Pass route to Sheffield, and the right fork leads to Glossop.

There are two viaducts on the line, and the first lies just beyond Broadbottom. The correct name for this viaduct is Besthill. It is the higher of the two at 136 feet, but is quite short. The Mottram marshalling yard lay just beyond here and some overgrown sidings can still be seen. Dinting viaduct took a year to build, and originally looked very different from the structure of today. It had laminated wooden arches which were replaced with plate girders in 1861, and the seven brick piers were added in 1918 as a means of strengthening the viaduct for the heavier freight traffic it was expected to carry. Once a busy junction, **Dinting** is now considerably reduced in importance. However the original Great Central Railway buildings remain, although only two of the four platforms are still used. Ahead the line curves to what was once the Woodhead route. Less than twenty-five years after the new Woodhead tunnel was constructed the line was the subject of a bitter battle against closure. Closure of the stretch beyond Hadfield finally took place in 1981.

Dinting Railway Centre is situated around the former Dinting locomotive depot, accessible from Dinting Lane. The Centre houses a number of large steam locomotives and industrial tank engines, with an engine in steam every Sunday from March to October. It is open every day from 10 a.m. to 5.30 p.m. On Mondays and Tuesdays the caretaker should be contacted in his caravan on the site, and a donation would be appreciated. On Wednesday to Saturday normal admission should be paid in the Centre shop at the rear of the exhibition hall.

The Glossop branch line has an interesting history. The line was built by the 13th Duke of Norfolk. As it was a private railway built on private land an authorising Act of Parliament was not required. Once a thriving cotton town, **Glossop** (population 25,000) is a gateway to the Peak District National Park. It has a number of tea shops and public houses, Friday and Saturday markets and some excellent shops. The station is a Grade II listed building. The proud Norfolk lion stands guard over the entrance used by the Duke and his family and the stone beneath him bears the date the station was opened for public use – 1847. On the right outside the station a small black and white timber building, originally a coal office, now houses the Information Centre. The volunteer staff within will give information on many subjects and there are also items for sale.

The road passing the station frontage rises out of the town and eventually joins the A628, passing alongside the west portal of Woodhead Tunnel before crossing into South Yorkshire. The A57 road through the centre of the town becomes the Snake Road over Ladybower and Derwent reservoirs, the scene of the practice runs for the Dam Busters raids. Access to the Pennine Way is possible from the Snake Pass. The A624 will take you to Hayfield and Chapel-en-le-Frith. For suitably equipped hikers Kinder and Edale can be reached from Glossop. Cycles can easily be carried on the electric multiple-unit trains, and the possibilities for cyclists in the area are almost endless.

The train travels to **Hadfield**, which was also a cotton town. Some of the cotton mills are still in use as factories and warehouses, but as in Glossop the bulk of them have been demolished. Station Road is the main shopping street, and a right turn onto the steep hill of Waterside leads to the aforementioned A628. Hadfield is the terminus of the line, and the train returns to Glossop before making the journey back to Manchester. The station building has been converted into a wine bar, and an extension has been constructed to house a new BR booking office and waiting room.

MANCHESTER–ALTRINCHAM

by Andrew Macfarlane

Our journey begins at **Manchester Oxford Road** Station which has undergone several rebuildings since its opening by the Manchester South Junction & Altrincham Railway in 1849. Its five platforms handle around 400 trains daily and its situation makes it convenient for much of the business area of the city. Our train heads out over the 'South Junction' viaduct which consists of 224 arches and contains no less than fifty million bricks. As we approach **Deansgate** Station we notice on our right the former Manchester Central station, now converted into the Greater Manchester Exhibition Centre or G-Mex for short. This is well worth a visit and a modern footbridge links Deansgate Station with the G-Mex site. The former Central station is now a listed building. Its roof was built to a similar design to London St Pancras and its span is only thirty feet shorter at 210 feet. Its maximum height is ninety feet above the former rail level.

Castlefield Junction, west of Deansgate, is where trains to Blackpool diverge to travel over the new 'Windsor Link' line. To our right we catch a glimpse of the buildings of Liverpool Road Station. This was the original terminus of the world's first inter-city railway, the Liverpool & Manchester, opened in 1830. Now restored, the station is the home of the Greater Manchester Museum of Science and Industry. The Castlefield Visitor Centre is nearby and there is a reconstruction of the Roman fort which stood underneath the course of the approach viaduct to Manchester Central. Looking down to our left we note the murky waters of the Bridgewater Canal below us. One of the first canals in the world when it opened in 1761, it is now used solely by pleasure craft as part of the 'Cheshire Ring' of canals. At Cornbook Junction we leave the main line to Liverpool via Warrington Central and after passing through **Old Trafford** tunnel, calling at the station and crossing over the closed Fallowfield loop freight line we see on our right Old Trafford Cricket Ground, the home of Lancashire County Cricket Club. **Warwick Road** Station is very conveniently situated for the cricket ground and is only a short walk from the equally famous home of Manchester United Football Club which has its own halt alongside the Manchester–Liverpool line.

After calling at **Stretford**, an important suburban station, our train heads through open country and crosses the River Mersey before passing under the M63 motorway. The lake to our left is the Sale Water Park which is popular with waterskiers and sailboard enthusiasts. It was formed when the ground was excavated to form the embankments of the motorway and the hole subsequently filled with water. After **Dane Road** Station we call at **Sale**, a station which retains much of its original character. The town of Sale is a pleasant, leafy suburb whose development owes much to the coming of the railway. The Town Hall, built in 1915, is an imposing structure and the former Odeon cinema is a good example of 1930s architecture. The former is situated diagonally opposite the station and the latter some ten minutes' walk away on the main A56. The nineteenth-century scientist J P Joule, who gave his name to the unit of work, was a resident of the town.

A short hop from Sale brings us to **Brooklands** Station, well-used by commuters and boasting a bookstall on the Manchester-bound platform. To our right beyond the canal after leaving Brooklands is Walton Park, which has its own miniature railway. A new station may be opened south of Brooklands after the conversion of the line to Light Rapid Transit, which is scheduled for completion in early 1992. **Timperley** is the next stop and an old building with canopy survives on the Manchester-bound platform. As with most stations on the line, the booking office is situated on the road overbridge. After Timperley we part company with the Bridgewater Canal which has run parallel since Stretford and pass under firstly the freight-only branch to Carrington and then the Skelton Junction to Warrington line which closed in July 1985. A large section of this line is scheduled to be converted into a cycleway by a company called Sustrans as part of an ambitious plan to link York and Liverpool. The newly-reopened line from Stockport joins us at Deansgate Junction and we call at **Navigation Road** Station, which opened with the original electrification of the Manchester–Altrincham line in 1931. The station is ten minutes' walk from the Altrincham Ice Rink where many famous skaters have trained. Note the surviving 'prefab' houses to our right as we leave the station. We pass under the Stockport Road flyover which replaced the former Altrincham North level-crossing and arrive at **Altrincham** Station, the terminus for our train. The busy town centre is a short walk away to our right.

MANCHESTER–NORTHWICH–CHESTER

by Andrew Macfarlane

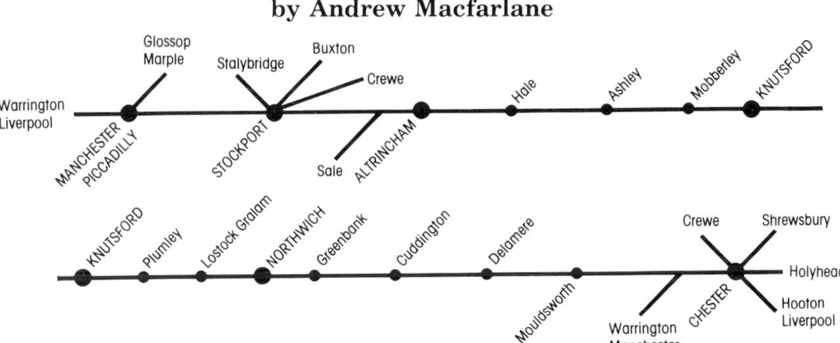

Our journey begins at **Manchester Piccadilly** Station. Since May 1989 trains to Chester via Northwich have started back from Warrington Central outside rush hours. We must therefore make our way to through platform 13 by means of the footbridge connecting the main part of the station with the through platforms. Prior to May 1989 Chester trains used the direct line to Altrincham through Sale but they now travel via Stockport and regain their previous route at Deansgate Junction, south of Timperley. Trains leave Manchester Piccadilly for Chester every hour in the off-peak period and the service is operated by a mixture of 'Sprinter' trains and conventional diesel multiple-units.

We take the fast line out of Piccadilly and pass through Levenshulme and Heaton Chapel stations without stopping. **Stockport** is our first port of call before we diverge from the main line to London at Edgeley Junction no. 2 signal-box, where pro-rail M.P. Peter Snape was once a signalman. The open space to our right was formerly the site of a steam locomotive depot, where the engine *Bahamas*, now at the Dinting Railway Centre, ended its days in British Rail service. The football ground beyond is the home of Stockport County F.C. To our left is Edgeley Junction no. 1 signal box, like no. 2 a reminder of the days of the London & North Western Railway, the company which owned our route as far as Northenden until 1923.

We now curve round to the right and the double track becomes single at Cheadle Village Junction, where a direct spur from Davenport on the Buxton line joined from the left. Our route was singled in the early 1970s in connection with the building of the M63 motorway so that only single-track bridges were required, a decision as short-sighted as similar line singlings such as Chester–Wrexham and Stockport–Denton. A new station may be built on our route at Cheadle Heath and doubling of the track out from Stockport would be necessary if that took place. At Cheadle Heath we cross over the former Midland Railway main line from London to Manchester, now a single track freight-only route at this point which is used by stone trains from the Peak District to Northwich and Widnes. We continue on a tree-lined embankment past the site of Cheadle LNW station closed in 1917 as a wartime economy measure. The site is marked by a coal depot on the right-hand side.

We pass under a series of motorway bridges and under the Styal line before our route again becomes double track. We then dive under yet another motorway bridge and see the Greater Manchester Waste Disposal Authority's refuse transfer station to our left. This is one of a number in the Greater Manchester area and all of Manchester's refuse is now taken out by rail to a disused quarry at Appley Bridge near Wigan. The line from Hazel Grove joins from our right and the tall Northenden Junction signal-box controls the junction. There is now no trace of the passenger station which lay beyond the road bridge but the former station goods yard survives as a cement terminal which receives traffic from Earles sidings near Hope in the Peak District.

Our route is now in a shallow cutting and predominantly straight as we thread the south Manchester suburbs and the northern edge of the Wythenshawe council estate, thought to be the largest municipal housing area in Western Europe. A new station may be opened to serve this area in the next few years. We pass through the Roundthorn Industrial Estate and the site of the former Baguley station, closed like Northenden in 1964, is marked by the porter's house to our right before we go under the main Altrincham to Stockport road and its predecessor. There is a loop line to our left before we swing to the right at Skelton Junction, once the focal point of the Cheshire Lines Railway and also controlled by a tall signal-box so that the signalman could see over the adjacent road bridge.

The line from here to Warrington is now completely closed and the Glazebrook line only remains open as far as Carrington to serve a Shell chemical plant. Our

A Chester–Manchester Oxford Road service crossing Leftwich Viaduct between Greenbank and Northwich. The Weaver Navigation is in the foreground. (*Photo*: Tom Heavyside)

train now takes a semi-circular curve around the site of a former marshalling yard before passing under the Glazebook and Warrington lines and joining the Manchester–Altrincham line at Deansgate Junction. To our right is an original Manchester South Junction & Altrincham Railway crossing keeper's cottage. Note the bells suspended above the roadway to warn drivers of high vehicles of the presence of the overhead wires over the level-crossing. This crossing is the first of four in succession which are the bane of motorists in the area.

At Navigation Road Station we note the former MSJ & A signal-box to our left and beyond the level-crossing to our right is some surviving 'prefab' housing. We pass under the flyover which replaced the level-crossing at Altrincham North and the signal-box of that name is to our left. The box is of London & North Western Railway origin and heralds our arrival at the neat four-platformed station which is our second stop. **Altrincham** is the terminus of the electric service from Crewe (via Manchester) although work will soon begin on conversion of the Altrincham–Manchester line to Light Rapid Transit which will provide direct access to the centre of Manchester. The new system is scheduled to be open in early 1992. Altrincham Station boasts a fine clock tower outside its forecourt, now a bus station. The town has a busy pedestrian-only shopping area which is connected by a footbridge to the bus-rail interchange. Tuesday and Saturday are market days at the traditional covered market in Shaws Road (turn left outside the station and first right). The town's non-league football ground is a short walk from the station in Moss Lane (left outside the station and first left).

Three miles south-west of Altrincham is the Georgian mansion of Dunham Massey which is open to the public from April to the end of October from 1 p.m. to 5 p.m. on every day except Friday. The surrounding 230-acre park is open daily. The hall was for over 300 years the seat of the Earls of Stamford and Warrington. More than thirty rooms in the hall are open to the public and there are fine collections of eighteenth-century furniture, portraits and Huguenot silver and a splendid Great Hall. In the garden visitors can sit on an Elizabethan mount, enjoy the sweet-scented myrtle in the orangery or wander alongside the Edwardian water garden. Bus services 37 and 38 run half-hourly from Altrincham to Warrington passing the entrance to the park.

Our train now winds its way out of Altrincham towards its next stop at **Hale**. Note the surviving semaphore signalling which is a feature of the line as far as Plumley West. We are now on the former Cheshire Lines Railway which was the largest jointly-owned railway company in Britain prior to nationalisation. Hale Station, originally known as Peel Causeway, is a fine example of Victorian railway architecture with its elaborate canopies and signal-box forming part of the station buildings. We leave Hale and pass Altrincham Boys Grammar School on our right before passing under an unusual single-arch road bridge which was necessary because of the skew angle of the road. We emerge into open country and cross the River Bollin which marks the boundary between Greater Manchester and the present county of Cheshire. **Ashley**, our next stop, is now unstaffed although its buildings remain. It was formerly known as Ashley for Rostherne, a picturesque village with an ancient church two miles to the west of Ashley.

Mobberley, also unstaffed, still has an operational Cheshire Lines signal-box controlling its level-crossing. The village of Mobberley is a mile to the south-east. We are now crossing what is known as the Cheshire Plain which provides some of the best farmland in the country due partly to the high rainfall. On our left we soon see in the distance the large new factory of Ilford Limited where photographic film and paper are made. We will also probably see an aircraft overhead on its way to or from Manchester International Airport, some five miles to the north-east.

New housing on our left heralds our approach to **Knutsford**. The Mid Cheshire Rail Users Association is campaigning for a new station to serve this area, known as Shaw Heath. We enter a cutting and to our right is a glimpse of some of the town's Italian-style buildings beyond the small lake known as the Moor Pool. To our left as we enter the station is another Cheshire Lines signal-box. The station was rebuilt in its present form in 1979 when the main entrance was moved from the Chester to the Manchester platform. The former main building is now in private hands but the canopy remains on the opposite platform to shelter waiting commuters. There are steep steps up to the main road bridge which cause problems for many passengers; the steps are in need of replacement by sloping ramps.

Knutsford (which gets its name from 'Canute's Ford' – legend has it that King Canute forded the River Lily here) is a most interesting historic town with many fine buildings including the Sessions House with its classical portico and nearby Tatton Hall, a stately home of 1813 designed by Samuel and Lewis Wyatt, which is open to the public. Every year there is the Royal May Queen Procession, which always attracts large crowds, many of whom come by rail. For more information on Knutsford see page 60. After Knutsford we cross the M6 motorway and arrive at **Plumley**, another unmanned station. Note the flower beds which are tended by the ladies of the Plumley Womens Institute. To our left after a short distance is Plumley West signal box, behind which is an underground brine field. Before passing under the Northwich bypass we pass the site of the closed Associated Octel chemical plant which made lead additive for petrol. **Lostock Gralam** is our next stop and the main building here is being converted into a private house. The waiting shelter on the opposite platform is in urgent need of attention.

After Lostock Gralam we cross over the Trent & Mersey Canal and to our right are several colourful narrow boats. It is possible to walk along the towpath of the canal to the historic Anderton Boat Lift which dates from 1874 and is currently being restored to its former glory. The lift, the only one of its type in Britain, raises boats fifty feet from the River Weaver to the Trent & Mersey Canal. As we approach Northwich the large Lostock Works of ICI, the town's largest employer, appear to our left. Note the old half-timbered house preserved in the midst of a modern chemical works. Extensive freight sidings on our left herald our arrival at **Northwich** Station where the opposite face of the island platform was once used by a service to Crewe via Middlewich. Note the former steam locomotive shed to our left, now awaiting an uncertain fate. After we have passed the triangular junction with the freight and diversionary route to Sandbach our train slows for Leftwich Viaduct, the most impressive engineering feature on this section of the line. It consists of forty-eight stone arches and two wrought-iron girder bridges and crosses the Rivers Dane and Weaver as well as the Weaver Navigation, the span of the bridge over the last being 110 feet. The total length of the viaduct is around 725 yards. To our right we have a good view of the town of Northwich with Northwich Victoria's football ground and the two road swing bridges over the Weaver Navigation prominent. Note the railway signals controlling entrance to the locks below us to the left. For more details on Northwich see page 60.

Immediately after the viaduct, the steeply-graded branch to ICI Winnington Works diverges to our right with the third side of the triangle trailing in before **Greenbank** Station, one of the busier on the line, which was refurbished for a visit by the royal train in May 1988. Hartford Station, on the Crewe–Liverpool line, is some twenty minutes' walk away. Our train enters a tree-lined cutting before passing Hartford CLC Junction where a freight-only spur leaves us to join the West Coast Main Line, which we cross over shortly afterwards. **Cuddington** Station is well-known for its rhododendron bushes which are at their best in May.

The station buildings too are worth a second glance, being in good external condition. The branch line which formerly ran from Cuddington to Winsford has for most of its length been converted into an interesting footpath known as the Whitegate Way after the line's intermediate station. It makes for a very pleasant walk, particularly in spring or autumn.

The line now passes through the prettiest scenery of the run as it skirts Delamere Forest and arrives at **Delamere** Station. There are a number of walks signposted through the forest which attracts visitors from a wide area. Picnic tables are provided at intervals and the forest is a haven of peace and quiet. Delamere Station is now unstaffed and the stone-built main building is in the process of conversion into a craft shop and café. The visitor centre at Linmere is nearby and the Sandstone Trail, a thirty-two mile walk from Frodsham to Grindley, can be joined in the area. **Mouldsworth** Station also boasts a fine display of rhododendrons as well as a timber Cheshire Lines signal-box controlling the junction with the single-track branch to Helsby West Cheshire Junction which is heavily used by oil trains from the refineries at Ellesmere Port. The station buildings at Mouldsworth are well-maintained and some railway cottages can be seen to our left behind the station.

Our train now enters a single-track section which extends as far as Mickle Trafford Junction. We pass the shell of Barrow for Tarvin Station, closed in 1953, on our right before joining the main Warrington to Chester line at Mickle Trafford. Note the single track heading off to our left. This was the original route to Chester Northgate Station, closed to passengers in October 1969 when the trains were diverted to their present terminus at Chester General. The line closed to freight in May 1984 but reopened in autumn 1986 to cater for increased freight traffic to Shotton steelworks on the banks of the River Dee. Mickle Trafford would be a good site for a new station in view of the recent housing development near to the line and the traffic problems of the city of Chester. Note the miniature railway with its semaphore signal on our right as we enter **Chester** Station and then the power signal-box which has controlled the station area since the early 1980s. Our journey ends in one of the bay platforms at the east end of the station. There are frequent bus services from outside the station to the Town Hall bus exchange in the city centre. For more information on Chester see page 58.

MANCHESTER–WARRINGTON–LIVERPOOL

by Andrew Macfarlane

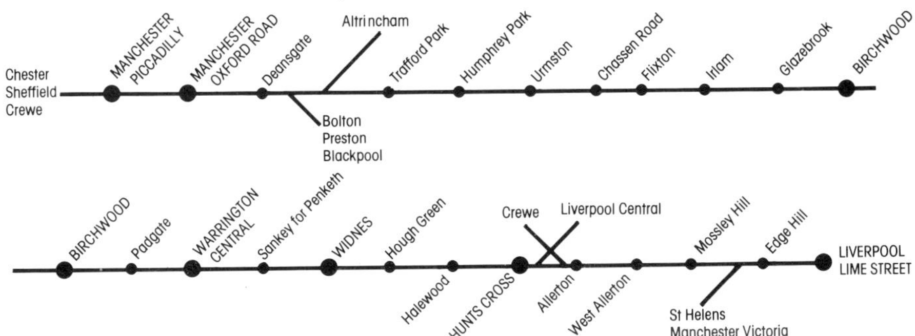

We begin our journey at **Manchester Piccadilly** Station from the rather wind-swept platforms 13 and 14, reached by connecting footbridge from the main station

Local train for Manchester Oxford Road at Glazebrook. (*Photo*: Tom Heavyside)

which was completely rebuilt with electrification of the main line to London Euston in the 1960s. Platforms 13 and 14 have now been rebuilt once again to take account of their increased role with the full commissioning of the 'Windsor Link' joining the previously separate rail networks of north and south Manchester. The island platform has been extended at its east end so that both platforms 13 and 14 can accommodate two trains at once and escalators and a lift make life easier for the traveller. The fast service from Manchester Piccadilly to Liverpool is now half-hourly. Our train will have either come from Sheffield via the Hope Valley route or from Leeds via Diggle and Guide Bridge. It will probably be formed of a class 156 'Super Sprinter' or, if it is one of the two-hourly Newcastle-Liverpool trains, locomotive-hauled carriages. Local trains also operate from Piccadilly to Warrington Central, every hour.

Our train sets out across the viaduct towards Oxford Road Station, passing the buildings of UMIST, the University of Manchester Institute of Science and Technology, on both sides of the line. The clock tower of the former Refuge Assurance building, a listed structure, heralds our arrival at **Oxford Road**, a very busy station for commuters. Leaving Oxford Road we pass the former Manchester Central Station on our right. Prior to 1969 our journey would have begun here.

We pass through **Deansgate** Station and veer off to the left at Castlefield Junction. At Cornbrook Junction we part company with the Altrincham line. The new Light Rapid Transit system will dive under our line at this point and make use of the former approach viaducts to Manchester Central to gain access to the centre of Manchester. Our speed rises as we pass the former Pomona Docks on our right and run parallel to the Bridgewater Canal. To our right is the Colgate Palmolive soap works and if we look upwards we can see the large mural by Rochdale artist Walter Kershaw depicting different aspects of Trafford Park. Beyond this can be glimpsed the refurbished Trafford Road bridge over the Manchester Ship Canal. To our right next is the Manchester United football ground with its own halt used by an electric shuttle service from Oxford Road on match days. Still on our right we see the Manchester International Freight Terminal (MIFT) which looks set to increase in importance with the opening of the Channel Tunnel. Beyond is the Trafford Park freightliner terminal through

42

which many hundreds of containers pass each year. There are daily services to Holyhead, Tilbury and Felixstowe among other destinations. Further on on our right is the new freight terminal for Pedigree petfoods which receives trainloads from Melton Mowbray. At **Trafford Park** Station we see to our right the GEC works, and the Kellogg factory where breakfast cereals are made. Soon afterwards we pass **Humphrey Park** Station, which was opened as a joint venture by British Rail, Greater Manchester Passenger Transport Executive and the former Greater Manchester Council in 1984. It serves a large residential area and has been a success in terms of numbers of passengers attracted to use the local train service. It would almost certainly have been more successful had the off-peak service been more frequent.

Urmston, 6 miles from Manchester, is an important station serving a quiet suburban town. **Chassen Road**, a small station opened in the 1930s, follows quickly as does **Flixton**, where the main building on the Warrington-bound platform has been converted into a pub-restaurant complete with its own foot-bridge linking the platforms. A steam generator has been installed at the base of this bridge in an attempt to recreate the atmosphere of the age of steam. Our train now begins the 1 in 135 climb to the bridge over the Manchester Ship Canal before Irlam Station. Note the locks to our right. To our left is Carrington Power Station which is rail-served and in the distance we can see the bridge which carried the Stockport to Glazebrook line (now closed) over the canal. The north bank of the canal here was formerly the site of a large steel plant which closed in the 1970s. The site is to be redeveloped as an industrial area with a new port facility. The construction of the canal in the 1890s necessitated diversion of the railway onto its present alignment. Thus **Irlam** Station is now 'the wrong way round', the tracks formerly passing on the other side of the main building.

Just before **Glazebrook** we see to our left the line from an oil terminal alongside the canal trailing in before we cross the River Glaze at Glazebrook East Junction and pass from Greater Manchester into Cheshire. The station buildings here are typical of the line. Note the railway cottages behind the Liverpool platform. Glazebrook was formerly an important junction with lines to Stockport and Wigan (from which line it was also possible to reach St Helens and the West Coast Main Line). There was a triangular junction with the Wigan line which was used for turning steam locomotives which had worked into the marshalling yard at Glazebrook East Junction. Traces of the triangle can be seen to our right as we head into open country and cross a former peat bog known as Risley Moss which was drained whilst the line was under construction in the 1870s. Part of the Moss is now a nature reserve administered by Cheshire County Council.

Our train slows for its second stop at **Birchwood**, a new station opened by the then British Rail chairman Sir Peter Parker in 1981 to serve the rapidly-expanding Warrington New Town. Bus services run from here to serve many parts of the new town. Leaving Birchwood we pass under the M6 motorway and come to **Padgate** Station, which is an architectural gem. West of here an avoiding line went off to our right which rejoined our route east of Sankey. This was used by express trains which did not stop at Warrington. Nowadays the town is too important a centre to ignore and **Warrington Central** is the line's busiest station.

Note the enormous goods warehouse on the right as we enter the station. Along the side are the names of the three railway companies which formed the Cheshire Lines Committee – the Midland Railway, the Great Central Railway and the Great Northern Railway. No longer in railway use, the listed structure is being converted for leisure use. The Cheshire Lines, which was known as 'the punctual railway' had its own signal works in Warrington. New street-level buildings were provided at Warrington Central in 1982 and the entire station has recently been refurbished to coincide with its increased importance as a call for Trans-Pennine services. For more details on Warrington see page 59. Leaving Warrington we cross over the West Coast main line and at Burtonwood we see to our right the connection to the former United States Air Force base, now administered by the US Army. This base became important during the second world war when at its peak 18,000 servicemen were stationed there. The site is now a giant warehouse housing $180 million worth of stores in case of war in Europe.

Sankey Station, like most on the line, retains its CLC station buildings. The full name of Sankey for Penketh still appears in timetables and since May 1988 the station has benefited from the increase in frequency of the local service from Warrington to Hunts Cross to half-hourly. We now enter open country and see to our left the eight massive cooling towers of Fiddlers Ferry power station, which receives most of its coal by rail. The next station, **Widnes**, was formerly known as Farnworth and later as Widnes North to distinguish it from the two stations in the town centre, both of which closed in the 1960s. Unlike at Warrington the loop line serving the town centre was closed leaving a station to serve the northern outskirts. The popular singer Paul Simon, of Simon and Garfunkel fame, wrote 'Homeward bound I wish I was . . .' whilst stranded at Widnes Station one night. The incident probably convinced him of the necessity to read timetables carefully!

Widnes (population 55,000) is famous for its chemical works and its Rugby League club. The town gets its name from 'wide-nose' which is nothing to do with any physical deformity in its inhabitants but refers to a wide nose of land in the Mersey estuary. The town was known as Runcorn Gap until the nineteenth century. The highly impressive Runcorn to Widnes road bridge links the town with the south bank of the Mersey. It replaced a transporter bridge, now demolished, in 1961; the transporter bridge is commemorated by a mural in the town centre. A smaller example survives at Warrington. Railway enthusiasts will be interested to learn that Widnes library contains a large collection of railway and transport publications.

Hough Green Station is served only by local trains but the station is well patronised, being the first from which cheaper Merseyrail fares are available! We next pass the new station of **Halewood**, opened in May 1988. There was once a marshalling yard to our right here in the triangular junction of the line to Aintree and Southport, now completely closed. **Hunts Cross**, $27\frac{1}{2}$ miles from Manchester, is the interchange station with the Northern line of Merseyrail and there are through electric services to Southport via Liverpool Central. It is to be hoped that the Liverpool–Warrington–Manchester line will benefit from 25 kV ac overhead electrification in the next ten years.

After Hunts Cross the third rail line to Liverpool Central diverges to our left and we pass the former Allerton motive power depot to our right. We join the main London–Liverpool line at **Allerton** Junction before passing the heavily-vandalised station of the same name. Our route is now four tracks wide and we soon pass **West Allerton** Station, like Allerton served only by the Liverpool to Crewe local service except during rush hours when there are through workings to and from Warrington Central. **Mossley Hill** is another suburban station before we curve round to the left, passing Edge Hill carriage sidings and joining the line from Manchester Victoria. Edge Hill was a favourite location for the famous railway photographer, Bishop Eric Treacy, the 'railway bishop'. Part of the original alignment of the Liverpool and Manchester railway can be seen to our left entering a steep cutting. A short length of this is still used for reversing freightliner trains. After **Edge Hill** Station we enter a series of tunnels and cuttings before arriving in Liverpool's main line terminal station, **Lime Street**, thirty-five miles from Manchester Piccadilly.

LIVERPOOL CENTRAL–HUNTS CROSS

by Andrew Macfarlane

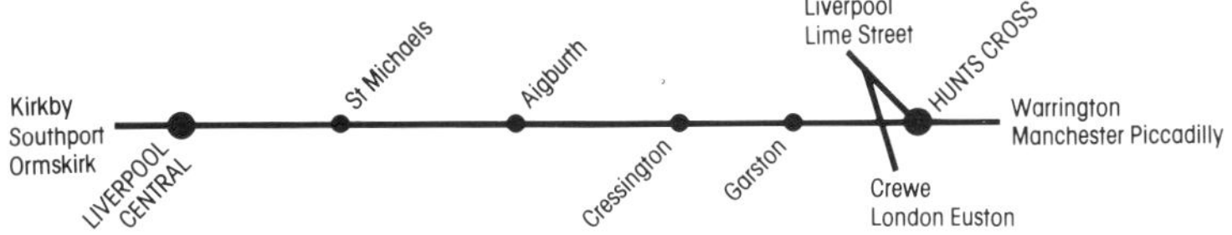

The story of this line is one of a phoenix-like revival after apparent final closure. Until September 1966 our route formed part of the main line from Liverpool Central to Manchester Central of the former Cheshire Lines Committee. From that date, however, the Manchester trains were diverted into Liverpool Lime Street Station and only the Liverpool–Gateacre local service remained on this section until it finally succumbed in April 1972. Thereafter most of the line was used only by an occasional train from Brunswick oil terminal, $1\frac{1}{2}$ miles from Liverpool Central. Liverpool Central Station itself was demolished even before the withdrawal of the Gateacre service and the other stations became increasingly derelict. However, Merseyside Passenger Transport Executive had plans for such a useful suburban route and the line was electrified with a third rail and incorporated in the Liverpool Link project, the Liverpool Central Low Level to Garston section reopening in 1978. The section from Garston to Hunts Cross was reactivated in 1983.

Our train will probably have come from Southport and will be one of the modern Class 507 or 508 electric multiple-units. Trains leave **Liverpool Central** for Hunts Cross every fifteen minutes in off-peak hours and every half-hour on Sundays. We depart and emerge from the Link tunnel only to pass through the four St James tunnels, all of which are about 200 yards long. We curve round to the left at the site of the former Brunswick locomotive depot and pass through Dingle Tunnel (1,082 yards long) to emerge into a cutting before **St Michaels** Station, our first stop. This was the nearest station to the 1984 Liverpool Garden Festival and new platform approach ramps were provided here by Marks & Spencer plc in view of the similarity of the station name to their trade mark. The CLC street-level building was renovated for the festival.

St Michaels Tunnel (103 yards long) follows before we traverse another cutting

Southport–Hunts Cross Merseyrail electric train at the restored Cressington Station. (*Photo*: Tom Heavyside)

and enter Fulwood Tunnel (200 yards long) after which we pass the disused platforms of Otterspool Station, closed in 1951. The next station, **Aigburth**, was known as Mersey Road and Aigburth until 1972. The short Grassendale Tunnel (76 yards long) follows before **Cressington** Station, which was restored to its former glory in time for its reopening and won awards from Europa Nostra and the Civic Trust. Note the former gas lamps converted to electric. Beyond Cressington a freight-only connection to Speke Junction on the Crewe–Liverpool line diverged until 1977. We curve to the left and arrive at **Garston** Station, a bus–rail interchange situated in leafy surroundings. The sixty-two-yard long Woolton Tunnel follows, and we pass under the main Euston–Liverpool line before we join the Liverpool Lime Street–Manchester Piccadilly line at Hunts Cross West Junction. **Hunts Cross**, $7\frac{1}{4}$ miles from Liverpool Central, is our terminus. A half-hourly connecting service runs from here to Warrington Central, calling at all stations.

WARRINGTON–CHESTER

by David Roberts

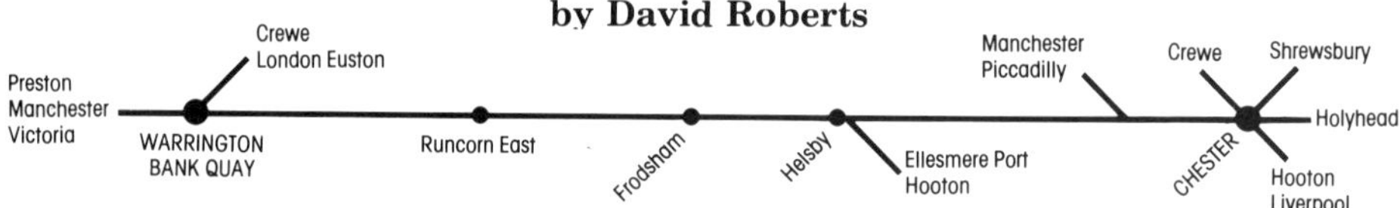

Warrington has been built on a wide range of industries such as metalworking, copper refining, wire making, tanning and soap manufacture. At the beginning of the nineteenth-century, goods via Liverpool were carried up and down the Mersey and landed at nearby Bank Quay, where large warehouses sprang up, marking it as an important trading port. Iron ships were built here in the 1850s. Today, Warrington has the distinction that more beer is brewed in and around it than anywhere else in Britain! (And a well-known brand of Vodka is distilled here.) The town centre has a new split-level shopping precinct, the Golden Square, linked with a bus interchange. A traditional covered market is still well used. To reach the centre from the station, cross the road by the Patten Arms Hotel and walk down one of the side streets for about 800 yards until one end of the shopping area is reached. **Warrington Bank Quay** Station is on the West Coast Main Line from Euston to Glasgow. The service to Chester is provided by 'Sprinter' diesel units operating from Stalybridge via Manchester Victoria.

We depart passing the River Mersey on the right where, due to improved pollution control, salmon have been seen. On the left is Arpley marshalling yard after which we cross over the Manchester Ship Canal. The peak year for traffic on the canal was 1958 and, after a decline in its use in the 1960s and 1970s, the canal is now undergoing something of a renaissance with new commercial traffic in prospect.

Out into open country now and the train leaves the cateneried main line at Acton Grange Junction. Before crossing over the main line, away to the left we may glimpse the buildings of the Atomic Energy Establishment at Daresbury. 'Lewis Carroll', otherwise known as the Reverend C. L. Dodgson, the author of *Alice in Wonderland*, spent much of his early life in Daresbury and there is a small museum dedicated to him in the village some three miles north-east of Runcorn East Station. (Buses between Warrington and Runcorn Shopping City serve Daresbury.) He is also commemorated by a window in the church depicting the caterpillar and the fish-footman.

Approaching the 'monopoly' style buildings of Runcorn New Town, we pass over the Duke of Bridgewater's Canal which ran from his coal-mines at Worsley, north-west of Manchester. **Runcorn East** is a well-designed and successful new station, opened in 1983 as a joint venture between British Rail, Cheshire County Council and the Warrington-Runcorn Development Corporation, to cater for the commuters and shoppers on the nearby housing estates. Immediately after setting off again, we enter a tunnel before emerging into a deep cutting and passing under the M56 motorway. The sides drop away as the freight line from Halton Junction, Runcorn joins us. There are fine views as the train runs over Frodsham Viaduct. Below is the River Weaver parallel with the Weaver Navigation Canal upon which rock salt from Northwich was once carried. Looking across to the right beyond the motorway is the Mersey estuary and shortly we arrive at our next stop.

Standing under the ridge of Overton Hill, **Frodsham** is an attractive, small town. The main road through the town is pleasantly wide and lined with trees. An old coaching inn, the Bear's Paw, stands here, built in 1632 out of sandstone with mullioned windows. A street market is still held, a custom going back to 1661. There are several cafés, pubs and a compact shopping centre. For walkers and ramblers, Frodsham is also the start of the 'Sandstone Trail', a path which runs for thirty-two miles across a diversity of Cheshire countryside and ends up at Grindley Brook on the Shropshire border.

Moving on, to the right we are looking out towards Frodsham Marshes, a wild and bleak place, popular only with wildfowl and ornithologists. After three miles, the train stops at **Helsby**. This is the terminus for the Helsby–Hooton–Chester shuttle (see Helsby to Hooton). There are always well-kept flower beds here, a credit to the station staff. Helsby itself is visibly noted for Helsby Hill, a craggy hill 462 feet high which is used as a practice ground for climbers. On its summit is part of an Iron Age promontory fort. There are wide views from the hill across the Mersey estuary and to the Welsh hills.

As the train draws away from Helsby, on the left can be seen the factory of British Insulated Callander's Cables which makes cable and wire products for the electronics industry. We carry on for the final seven miles, passing under the single freight line from West Cheshire Junction to Mouldsworth Junction. After running through a couple of cuttings, we pass over the little River Gowy which empties into the Mersey and join with the Northwich line of Mickle Trafford Junction. The freight line to Shotton steelworks, six miles west of Chester, passes over us and we descend a fairly steep incline for the last couple of miles. We join the Crewe line on the left as we finally run into **Chester** Station. For more details on Chester see page 58.

HELSBY–HOOTON

by David Roberts

This nine-mile link, built in 1863, is primarily a freight line for the large petro-chemical plants and other industries strung along the Manchester Ship Canal on the south side of the Mersey estuary. The passenger service provided runs to and from Chester and the elderly diesel multiple-units have been replaced by the Class 142 'Pacer' railbus. The service is half-hourly on Monday to Saturday but there are no trains on Sunday.

We start our journey at **Helsby** (described in the Warrington to Chester route).

Busy scene at Stanlow & Thornton with a diesel multiple unit from Rock Ferry being passed by an oil train. (*Photo*: Tom Heavyside)

Moving off, we run the two miles to **Ince and Elton**, passing under the M56 motorway and, on the right, Ince 'B' power station. Ince UKF Shellstar fertilizer factory, also to our right, provides significant freight traffic for BR in the form of block trains to many parts of the country. The unstaffed station is located at Elton, a mainly modern village with a small shopping precinct, situated on the left of the line. A half-mile away in the opposite direction is the isolated little village of Ince. The name comes from the Welsh *ynys*, meaning an island. To the west is a wall of oil storage tanks and, to the north, the Manchester Ship Canal. After the pub on the right a lane runs down towards Ince Marshes, past the sandstone ruins of the medieval hall, the lord of which was the abbot of St Werburgh's of Chester. A mile further on is **Stanlow and Thornton**. This halt is in the middle of about three square miles of oil refining and storage complexes and the footbridges on the platforms lead away to the works. Passing the lines of tanker wagons we trundle on two miles to the next stop.

Ellesmere Port was named as the terminus of the Ellesmere Canal scheme originating from the town of Ellesmere in Shropshire. It was part of a grand but ill-fated plan to link the Mersey, Dee and Severn. Nevertheless, the link from Chester was cut in 1795. After the building of the Birmingham & Liverpool Junction Canal in 1835 trade increased greatly and the connection of the Manchester Ship Canal in 1891 turned the town into an important transport centre. This century saw the arrival of the Shell oil refinery in 1922, the Bowater's Paper Company in the 1930s and Vauxhall Motors in the 1950s. The modern town centre is to the left of the station about 800 yards along the main road. A big attraction is the National Waterways Museum.

The museum is based within the once-thriving Shropshire Union dock complex and has won the Council of Europe 'Museum of Europe' award. Apart from housing the world's largest collection of traditional canal boats there are restored 1830s cottages and eight indoor exhibitions. Boat restoration can be seen in progress and the pump house contains restored steam engines which once powered forty cranes. Boat trips can also be taken along the Shropshire Union Canal and ships can be seen moving down the Manchester Ship Canal. The museum is open daily from April to October from 10 a.m. to 5 p.m. and from November to March daily except Fridays from 11 a.m. to 4 p.m. To get to the museum, turn right out of the station (a small hut here sells tea and snacks), past the Station Hotel and it is 800 yards along the road just after passing under the elevated motorway.

Moving on through a long cutting, we next call at the new station at **Overpool**, opened in August 1988, and then come to **Little Sutton**, a station set amongst housing estates although there is a small shopping centre on the main Birkenhead to Chester road which is 200 yards on the left out of the station. After entering another cutting, the line curves to the right as we cover the last mile and a half emerging at **Hooton**. Here we may stay on to Chester or change over to the Merseyrail train for Birkenhead or Liverpool. The line from Ellesmere Port to Hooton is shortly to be electrified, with commissioning due for 1991. This will provide a through service from Ellesmere Port to Liverpool and should boost the line's patronage.

CHESTER–LIVERPOOL
by David Roberts

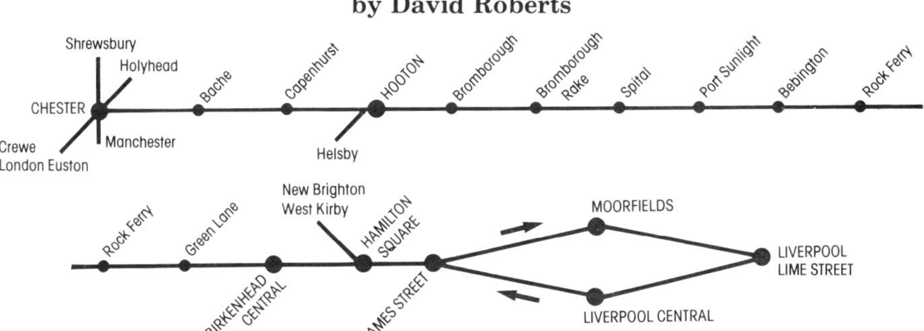

This line runs for fifteen miles up the east side of Wirral, and continues under the Mersey estuary to Liverpool. The line from Chester to Hooton is shortly to be electrified, enabling through electric trains to run from Chester to Liverpool from 1991.

We leave **Chester** and run through the suburbs to the first stop, the **Bache**. The name comes from the Middle English meaning 'stream in a valley'. This halt opened in early 1984 as a more convenient location to replace the old Upton-by-Chester station. Chester Zoo is a mile and quarter away. Emerging into open country, we pass over the Shropshire Union Canal. The train runs through a shallow cutting for about one and a half miles to emerge at **Capenhurst**, a halt serving the British Nuclear Fuels factory on the left. Capenhurst was mentioned in the Domesday Book as 'Capeles', part of the grant to William Fitznigell, Baron of Halton. We run on for three miles to the next stop.

Hooton Station marks the present boundary of the Merseyrail system with a bus/rail interchange and highly successful 'park and ride' car park. We must change here and board the third rail electric train. The station stands with an inn midway between the village of Willaston, a mile to the west, and Hooton, to the east. Willaston has an inn dating from 1631 and the remains of one of the brick windmills which were once common on Wirral. Hooton is also a junction for the branch line to Helsby which connects there with the main line to Warrington.

In 1956 the last passenger train ran the twelve miles from West Kirby to Hooton. Today this single-track line has been transformed into 'the Wirral Way' pathway. Besides giving superb views across the Dee estuary to the Welsh hills, there are picnic areas, a Country Park Visitor Centre and restored station buildings at Hadlow Road, just over a mile from Hooton. To gain access to the pathway, turn left after leaving the station, walk over the bridge and follow the signed footpath immediately on the left.

Three's company at Hooton Station with, from left, Merseyrail electric train to Liverpool, preserved Liverpool–Southport electric train and diesel multiple unit train on the Helsby–Chester service. (*Photo*: Tom Heavyside)

As the train glides quietly away, we pass under the M53 motorway and after about a mile and half come to **Bromborough**, a residential area. The train has hardly set off again before we come to **Bromborough Rake**, a very well-used new station which was suggested by the Bebington Rail Action Group. On the left, a footpath leads into a wooded area. After another short hop the train rises onto an embankment to **Spital**. The name is derived from a house of ho-spital-ity founded by William Lancelyn in 1170. Continuing on, the vast factory complex of Unilever is visible on the right and, after a mile, we are at **Port Sunlight**. William Hesketh Lever founded the model village named after his famous product, Sunlight Soap, in 1888. The impression is one of well-designed 'cottages' in very spacious areas. The Lady Lever Art Gallery is about a fifteen-minute walk from the station. This building contains a magnificent collection of paintings, furniture, Wedgwood Pottery and China porcelain. The best way to tour the village is to start at the Port Sunlight Heritage Centre (cross underneath the lines and turn right, 150 yards on left). You can buy a souvenir bar of soap here if you wish!

Passing the 'village' on the right, a mile further along is **Bebington**, a suburban station. Another mile on and we pause at **Rock Ferry**. This was the old terminus of the Merseyrail electric trains before the opening of the extension to Hooton. Moving on, we glimpse on the right the shipbuilding yards of Cammel-Laird. Famous names that have slid down the slipway are *Ark Royal* (two), *Mauretania* and *Prince of Wales*. The line now sinks to the semi-subterranean suburban **Green Lane** Station and heads into a tunnel to emerge half a mile further on at **Birkenhead Central**. Across from the station is the Grange, a large shopping precinct. Birkenhead was famous as having the first tramway in Europe in 1860 along with Birkenhead Park, the first public park in the country to be funded by the ratepayers. The Boy Scout movement was inaugurated in Birkenhead in 1908.

The train re-enters a tunnel for our last half mile to the underground station of **Hamilton Square**. At Hamilton Square we can change trains for New Brighton or West Kirby, carry on through the tunnel to Liverpool or go out via the lift.

Leaving the station, the Woodside landing stage for the ferry across the Mersey can be seen on the left behind the bus terminal. If you turn right and walk up towards the town hall, you will see Hamilton Square, a well-kept public garden surrounded by office buildings built in 1847. Thomas Brassey, the celebrated railway engineer, who built the Lancaster & Carlisle Railway over Shap, spent his early adult life in Birkenhead.

LIVERPOOL–WEST KIRBY
by Alan McGiffin

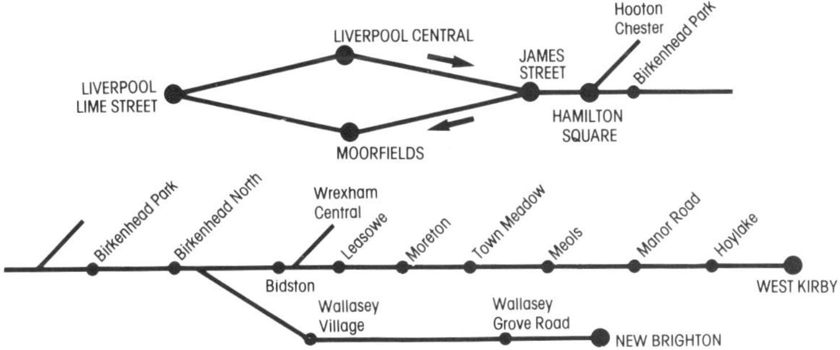

Our journey begins at **Moorfields** Station on the Liverpool Loop line, opened in 1977. The Wirral Line trains use a modern single platform which is linked by a passage and escalator with the Northern Line platforms. **Lime Street Low Level**, the next station, is similar to Moorfields and provides an interchange with services from the main line station. **Central Deep Level** is another interchange with the Northern Line services which run from its low level platforms. Just after Central

West Kirby–Liverpool electric train leaving Bidston. (*Photo*: Tom Heavyside)

the old route to Low Level (used before the opening of the Loop) can be seen on the right. Empty stock workings to and from the Northern Line still use this connection. At **James Street** the old inward platform is now dimly-lit but can still be used in emergencies.

Leaving James Street we enter the 100-year-old Mersey Railway tunnel under the river, encountering a 1 in 45 gradient, one of the steepest on the BR system. **Birkenhead Hamilton Square** retains its distinctive original building at street level, reached by lift from the platforms. After Hamilton Square our train dives under the Hooton line and emerges from the tunnel at **Birkenhead Park**, which also retains some of its original buildings. We then travel through cuttings to **Birkenhead North** Station, once called Birkenhead Docks. This three-platformed station still has much character. Note the Wirral Railway horn symbol on the main building. Leaving Birkenhead North we see on the right a large BR maintenance depot which services the Merseyrail electric fleet. Soon the New Brighton branch can be seen curving off sharply to the right.

Approaching Bidston, a now-closed double track spur trails in on the right, a former link from Seacombe Junction on the New Brighton line. **Bidston** Station is the terminus for the DMU services from Wrexham. Note the large Dee Junction signal-box on the right as we leave the station. The next station, **Leasowe**, is one of the busiest on the line, being a bus-rail interchange. The level-crossing signal-box is still manned and the gates are open and shut by hand. Between Leasowe and Moreton can be seen the large Cadbury factory on the right. **Moreton** signal-box remains open and leaving the station we pass a former brickworks on the right. The site of the long-awaited **Town Meadow** Station can be seen where the line crosses the Arrowe Brook. **Meols** Station is on the main West Kirby to Birkenhead road, in an attractive situation adjacent to a large pond. The layout is similar to Moreton's with the main building on the overbridge.

Manor Road is one of the neatest stations on the line with a pleasant open aspect to the south. **Hoylake** Station, the original Wirral Railway terminus, was rebuilt by the LMS in 1938 and possesses one of the largest station buildings on the line. The level crossing is controlled by the signal-box. Hoylake has a pleasant promenade similar to that at West Kirby. The shore is rather muddy but the air is bracing and there are good views of the Mersey estuary and the North Wales coast.

Leaving Hoylake, Grange and Caldy Hills and the Welsh Mountains can be seen on the left. The imposing war memorial on Grange Hill was constructed in 1921 and the 'Mariners' Beacon' on Caldy Hill was built as a marker for Mersey shipping in 1840. The red-brick, two-platform station at **West Kirby** has recently been modernised but its original character is still apparent. Turning left from the station, visitors who can manage the stiff half-mile climb (or take the now-infrequent bus) will be rewarded by some fine views from Grange and Caldy Hills. To the north can be seen Liverpool and the Mersey estuary and, on a clear day, Blackpool Tower and the Cumbrian Hills. To the west there is a panorama of the Dee and Clwyd with the Snowdonia range in the distance.

The former West Kirby to Hooton line is now the Wirral Way linear country park with a twelve-mile walk to Hooton via Heswall and Neston. It is also possible to walk the nine miles from West Kirby to Parkgate past some of the last red-clay cliffs in Britain. The promenade and marine lake (now being reconstructed) are only 200 yards from the station. Three small tidal islands can be seen about two miles across the sands to the north-west. These can be reached at low tide but attention to tide times, route and weather conditions is essential. An old pair of shoes should be worn to avoid cut feet from broken glass and sharp rocks. A permit, obtainable from 'The Concourse' adjacent to West Kirby Station, is required to visit the largest island, Hilbre. On Hilbre is a permanent bird observation and ringing station and over 200 species have been recorded there. Swimming in the vicinity of the islands is not recommended and it should be noted that there are no facilities and little shelter. An easier walk is available along the shore to Red Rock Point and Hoylake (around 1½ miles). Hilbre appears to be temptingly close to the Red Rocks but the crossing from here and from Hoylake is very dangerous.

BIRKENHEAD NORTH–NEW BRIGHTON
by Alan McGiffin

This short but busy branch leaves the West Kirby line at Bidston East Junction by a sharp curve to the right. At Seacombe Junction the closed curve from Bidston joins on the left and the parallel branch to Bidston Docks diverges to the right. The first station, **Wallasey Village**, is a modern structure situated on an embankment alongside a dual carriageway road. Less than a mile further on is the older **Grove Road** Station which still has some of its original buildings. **New Brighton** itself has a smart two-platform station similar to that at West Kirby. Note the fine Wirral Railway signal-box on the left as we enter the station.

New Brighton was once a popular seaside resort, particularly for day trippers. It had its own football league side and even a tower taller than Blackpool's. The tower, constructed between 1897 and 1900, was a slender lattice-work finger of steel rising 621 feet above sea level and was the highest structure in Britain until its demolition in 1919–21.

Today New Brighton is rather run-down with its pier and ferries just a memory. However, a pleasant walk may still be had along the promenade and there are interesting views of the Liverpool river-front and Mersey estuary. The restored fort on Perch Rock, built in 1827 along with the lighthouse as a defence for Liverpool, is well worth a visit. Visitors with energy to spare can walk the two-and-a-half miles to Seacombe along the traffic-free promenade and return to Liverpool by ferry. It is even possible to walk the 10 miles along the promenade and sea wall all the way from Seacombe to Hoylake, apart from a gap of a few hundred yards.

BIDSTON–WREXHAM
by Michael Barber and John Edge

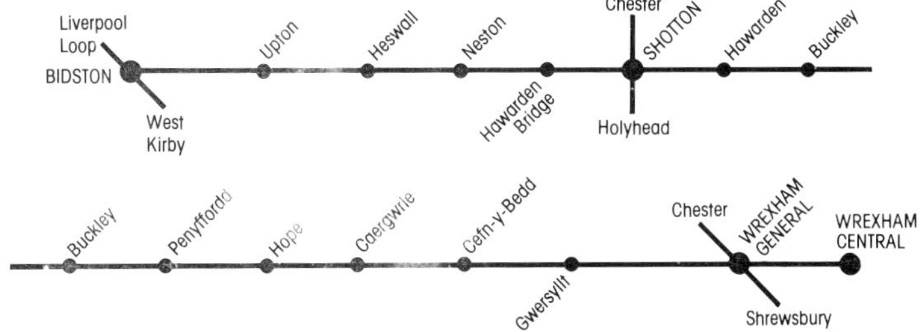

The northern terminus of this line, opened throughout by the Wrexham, Mold & Connahs Quay Railway in 1896, was changed from Birkenhead North to Bidston in 1979. It is hoped to return to Birkenhead North before long, it being much more convenient for connections with Merseyrail. However, it is currently from **Bidston** Station that we start our journey on the 'Friendly Line' as it has become

A Bidston–Wrexham Central train at Wrexham General Station. The platforms for the Chester–Shrewsbury service can be seen to the right. (*Photo*: Tom Heavyside)

known. Soon the wooded slopes of Bidston Hill may be seen to the left, with the two black domes of the tidal observatory from which all Britain's tidal movements are documented. A little further along the hilltop is Bidston windmill and the hill is full of colour each spring with its display of rhododendrons.

We are soon at **Upton** Station, or rather the remains of it. At least the far-from-picturesque submarine-pen-style concrete shelter on the Bidston platform has defied the local vandals to date. We start to climb and curve right as we pass Prenton Golf Course and the M53 motorway passes over the line. Some new housing has been constructed near **Heswall** Station recently and this will hope-fully boost the line's custom. The stretch between Heswall and Neston commences with fairly deep wooded cuttings followed by some fairly sharp curves. Close by the track on the left we pass the factory of the Morgan Refractories Group and soon we draw into **Neston** Station, one of the few on the line to retain any of its original buildings. Neston is also one of the busiest stations on the line and it is favoured as a place for a future Merseyrail electric terminus.

Very soon after leaving Neston we cross over the trackbed of the Hooton to West Kirby line, now the Wirral Way linear country park. As the train picks up speed on the descent, really lovely views across the Dee estuary may be seen to the right, views not enjoyed by road travellers on Wirral. On the left may be seen the western extremities of **Ness Gardens** which are well worth a visit on a nice day at any time of the year. Buses operate from near Neston station to Ness Gardens. A deep cutting takes us through solid sandstone and, on emerging onto the wide open fields beyond, look back to see that the train has just burst through what were once cliffs on the shore line of an estuary.

The sidings we now pass on the right serve the recently extended Deeside Paper Mill. Trains of timber from Scottish fir plantations are the main input to the sidings, and finished paper is now taken out by rail. On our left can now be seen the Deeside Titanium Plant, the only one of its kind in Europe which produces the specialist metals used in aero engines. The tank wagons in its sidings have usually come from the Continent via the train ferry. At Dee Marsh Junction the freight-only line to Mickle Trafford which reopened in September 1986 curves away to the left. As our train takes a tight curve to the right, the sidings alongside are used for the reception of coiled steel for the BSC Coating and Finishing Mill, the highly successful remnant of the once massive Shotton Steelworks. Dee Marsh Junction signal-box to our right is of Great Central Railway origin.

Hawarden Bridge Station is our next stop. Immediately the station is left, the train is crossing the Dee. Nearly a hundred years old, the swing bridge, which is now incapable of swinging, was once the biggest of its kind in the world. Soon we cross over the main Crewe to Holyhead line, where we see the low level platforms of **Shotton** Station to the right, and arrive at one of the high level platforms. There is a proposal to instal one or more curves at Shotton to link the Crewe to Holyhead line with the Bidston to Shotton route. This would enable a Bidston to Chester passenger service to be operated and would release the Mickle Trafford line for possible conversion to Light Rapid Transit. As the train leaves Shotton we begin the climb at 1 in 53 to the village of Hawarden. From the left-hand side a magnificent view over the Cheshire Plain may be had. This section of line was opened in 1890 to bypass the original, steeply-graded and tightly-curved route through the village of Buckley.

Points of interest in **Hawarden** (pronounced Harden) include the Clwyd County Record Office, the thirteenth-century parish church and the castle. Hawarden Station is by far the best-kept on the line, this being due to the tireless efforts of Mr Bill Roberts, who acts as its voluntary caretaker. New housing has recently been built in the former station goods yard here also. On leaving Hawarden, the line continues its ascent at 1 in 53 to reach the summit at **Buckley** Station, formerly Buckley Junction. Leaving Buckley the line descends, passing on the right the Padeswood works of Castle Cement, with its extensive sidings. The train draws into **Penyffordd** Station, where a branch leaves to the west to serve the cement works.

Leaving Penyffordd, the train traverses open country with fine views to the right of Hope Mountain, reaching in due course **Hope** Station. Hope is closely followed by **Caergwrle** Station. Caergwrle is an interesting village, being developed in the early years of this century as a spa in an attempt to rival the famous Victorian spa towns. Remains of the wells and associated mineral water bottling plant still exist in the woods along the far bank of the River Alyn which flows to the east of the station. The ruined castle, built by Edward I on top of the wooded hill directly to the west of the station, is worth a visit.

The train soon proceeds to the third of three closely-spaced stations, **Cefn-y-bedd** (Welsh for 'beyond the grave'!). Just south of Cefn-y-bedd the line crosses the major civil engineering feature of the line – a fine stone viaduct over the River Cegidog. Below the viaduct and to the right is an unusual restored water mill. South of Cefn-y-bedd Viaduct the line runs along a hillside affording extensive views eastwards towards the Cheshire Plain. Soon **Gwersyllt** Station is reached and if you look beyond the station you will notice the line makes a sharp dip. This was to pass under the now long-gone North Wales Mineral Railway of 1846. One mile south of Gwersyllt we pass under the Wrexham bypass and run alongside the Chester to Shrewsbury line, which is described in *Wales and the Marches by Rail*.

The train now enters a single-track section before entering **Wrexham General** Station, the Bidston platforms of which were formerly known as Wrexham Exchange. The single track dives down after Wrexham General and curves tightly to the left before we reach our terminus at **Wrexham Central** Station. So finishes our journey of $27\frac{1}{2}$ miles, traversing two countries and three counties – there can be few lines which incorporate so much variety and interest in such a short distance!

BUXTON

by Felix Schmid

The Romans were the first to develop Buxton as a spa, calling it, appropriately, Aquae Arnemetiae. The name Buxton means 'logan' or 'rocking stones' and the thirteenth-century form was 'Bucstanes'. The good waters of Buxton were rediscovered by the 5th Duke of Devonshire. Realising the tourist potential, between 1780 and 1786 he built the Crescent, a magnificent curved building designed by John Carr of York housing the baths and the pump room, where patients could have a surprisingly good-tasting drink or treat their rheumatism in the naturally hot spring water. The Duke also built himself a riding school, now a hospital, featuring what was then the largest free-span dome in the world, with a diameter of 150 feet.

A tour of Buxton (population 21,000) may start with the Crescent (where we find the tourist information office), the baths and the micrarium, an award-winning museum of semi-precious stones. From there a mile's walk brings us to the top of Grin Low and to Solomon's Temple, a nineteenth-century folly with a good view of Buxton and the surrounding heights. Nearby, we find Poole's cavern. The walk back from this curiosity takes us through the Pavilion Gardens with its miniature railway and we may even have a look at the exquisite Opera House, a miniature version of the Scala in Milan. A visit follows, perhaps, to the Duke of Devonshire's Hospital to admire the dome (please respect the quiet of the place) before we stop for afternoon tea at the Pavilion, which also has a dome and dates from 1871.

Short trips by bus take in Castleton and the Blue John mines. Slightly longer journeys reach Bakewell or Matlock and the Heights of Abraham. Both the Tissington and High Peak Trails start just outside Buxton and are ideal for walks as well as cycle rides far from the roads. Earl Sterndale, Wolfcote Dale and romantic Dove Dale are close at hand, only a few miles south of Buxton.

The Crescent, Buxton.

STOKE-ON-TRENT

by Andrew Macfarlane

The Potteries cover an area ten miles long and between two and three miles wide. The 'Five Towns' of Arnold Bennett's novels are in fact six – Longton, Fenton, Stoke, Hanley, Burslem and Tunstall. These six were united in 1910 to form the borough (now city) of Stoke-on-Trent. Rough brown pottery was made at Burslem before the end of the sixteenth century but the industry received its first great impetus in 1715 with the introduction of purer clays from Devon and Cornwall. Josiah Wedgwood first established a factory at Etruria in 1769. The area was thus named under the erroneous impression that the classical vases which he copied came from Etruria. The main reason for the development of pottery-making in the locality was the abundance of coal for firing the kilns and all of the ingredients used came from outside the immediate area – china clay from Devon and Cornwall, ball clay from Dorset, flints from Norfolk and felspar from Derbyshire.

Today electricity has replaced coal as the principal means of firing the kilns. The Wedgwood factory is now at Barlaston, south of Stoke, and has a visitors' centre which includes the Wedgwood museum housing examples of ware from the eighteenth to the twentieth centuries and of Josiah Wedgwood's experimental pieces. The centre is open from Monday to Saturday from 9 a.m. to 4 p.m. and is adjacent to Wedgwood Station on the Stoke–Stafford line. The sturdy and intelligent character of the music-loving inhabitants of the Potteries was vividly described in the novels and stories of Arnold Bennett. Stoke was his 'Knype' and is the railway centre of the Potteries. Adjacent to the station entrance in Winton Square is The Potteries Centre, a pottery factory shop. 'Potters Round' guided mini-bus tours start from here during the summer months and full details can be obtained from the Tourist Information Office (Tel. 0782-411222).

If we turn right under the railway bridge and walk over the bypass road and the Trent & Mersey Canal we come to the Town Hall in Glebe Street which contains the tourist information office, open Monday to Friday. The Spode china factory, shop and museum are just around the corner in Church Street. The museum, which is open from Monday to Friday from 9 a.m. to 4 p.m., contains early collections and incorporates an old 'bottle oven'. Josiah Spode perfected a blue transfer printing process on to earthenware in 1784 and went on to discover the formula for bone china, prized ever since for its delicacy, whiteness and translucence.

A short bus ride from Stoke Station brings us to Hanley, the main shopping centre of the Potteries and the most populous of the six towns. Hanley was the birthplace of Arnold Bennett, who spent his early childhood at 205 Waterloo Road, Cobridge, which is now a museum dedicated to him. The Museum and Art Gallery in Broad Street, Hanley, contains the world's largest collection of Staffordshire figures and other ceramics and is open from 10 a.m. to 6 p.m. from Monday to Saturday and from 2.30 to 5 p.m. on Sundays. The first floor is dedicated to an exhibition of English watercolours.

A 90 or a 92 bus from Longport Station will take us to the centre of Burslem and the Royal Doulton factory, renowned for its tableware and figures. There are factory tours, a magnificent museum and a factory shop. A 96 or 97 bus from Longport will take us to the Chatterley Whitfield Mining Museum where you can go underground and experience life down a pit a century ago. There are pit ponies and, on the surface, working locomotives and winding gear. The pit canteen and giftshop can also be visited.

There are four ceramic factory shops within easy reach of Longton Station on the Stoke–Derby line. A traditional early-Victorian Potbank Yard in Uttoxeter

Road, Longton, has been carefully restored as a working museum of the trade, called the Gladstone Pottery Museum, which is open daily from March to October and daily except Monday, Christmas Day and Boxing Day from November to February. From Longton Station walk up Market Street, the other side of the roundabout, to Uttoxeter Road, where the museum is on the right. As with many of the attractions of the Potteries, there is a twenty per cent discount on the admission charge for rail ticket holders.

CHESTER

by David Roberts

Founded by the Romans, Chester (population 58,000) is a blend of a city steeped in history and an extensive shopping centre. *Valeria Victrix*, the crack XX Legion, made Chester or Deva (after the goddess of the River Dee) their headquarters in the first century. Where the four original main roads of the Roman camp once ran are now the four main streets of Northgate, Eastgate, Watergate and Bridge Street. The remains of the amphitheatre, the largest discovered in Britain, and the Roman garden are displayed in the south-east corner of the city by the walls. A complete ring of medieval defensive walls and towers surrounds the inner city and a walk around the ramparts is well worth the experience.

In the early tenth century, a church was founded on the site of the present cathedral in which were placed the relics of St Werburgh. The church was turned into a Benedictine abbey in about 1093 and the cathedral today is the abbey church, restored in the medieval style in the nineteenth century. The choir stalls have become famous because of their beautifully carved canopies, corbels, bench-ends and misericords.

A new attraction in Chester is the St Mary's Centre, alongside County Hall. The centre, formerly the Church of St Mary's-on-the-Hill, is a treasure-house of English history and architecture, including medieval stained glass, a fifteenth-century wall painting, the sixteenth-century nave roof and the seventeenth-

The corner of Northgate Street, Chester.

century Gamul and Oldfield family tombs. There are also temporary exhibitions and the centre is a venue for concerts, literary events, lectures and conferences. Public viewing takes place from 2 p.m. to 4.30 p.m. from Monday to Friday although the centre is closed on bank holidays and throughout August.

Other features of the city are the unique 'Rows', covered medieval walkways at first floor level. The 'black and white' timbered buildings are mainly nineteenth-century for several are sixteenth or seventeenth century in origin, one of the most interesting being Bishop Lloyd's House in Watergate Street. Where the city walls bridge over Eastgate Street, stands the ornate Diamond Jubilee Clock of 1897. Throughout the year there are guided tours of Chester. Two unusual ones are the 'Ale Trail', visiting historic inns and taverns, and the 'Ghosthunter Trail', a night-time journey around the eerie haunts of the city. These, and other tours, start from either the tourist information centre by the Town Hall or Chester visitors' centre in Vicar's Lane. Chester was the most important port in the north-west of England up to medieval times and where the Roodee racecourse now stands was the Romans' harbour. Cruises can be taken on the River Dee and boats hired. A regatta, river carnival and raft race are held every year.

Chester Zoo, on the outskirts of the city, contains a wide range of mammals, birds, reptiles and fish in its 100 acres of landscaped gardens. The zoo is the largest in Britain outside London and houses many rare and endangered species. The famous chimp island is home to the biggest group of chimpanzees in the country. There is also one of the finest tropical houses in Britain, containing many exotic trees and plants, a superb reptile collection and colourful tropical birds. There are free guided tours and you can even make a brass rubbing of your favourite endangered species. Young visitors can make a mask, a model, a puppet or a painting. In the summer there is a waterbus service and the zoo is accessible to the disabled. It is open from 10 a.m. until dusk every day except Christmas Day. Buses run from the Town Hall Bus Exchange (four an hour) and also from the railway station to the zoo. It is about twenty minutes' walk from Bache Station.

WARRINGTON

by Andrew Macfarlane

The town of Warrington owes its development to its key position as for many years the most westerly crossing point of the River Mersey before the river begins to widen into an estuary. Its history stretches back at least to the Bronze Age and the Romans had a settlement at Wilderspool on the south bank of the river which they called Veratinum. The first record of a bridge is in 1305 and by the end of the eighteenth century Warrington was developing as an industrial centre, tanning and brewing and the making of copper and wire being the main activities. Wire manufacture and brewing remain important today. Soap manufacture began in 1815 and still continues, a large works being situated alongside the main London–Glasgow line at Bank Quay Station.

Today the town centre, which is within easy walking distance from both Bank Quay and Central stations, boasts a pleasant, pedestrianised traditional shopping area and the modern Golden Square split-level precinct, close to Central Station, with a bus station beneath. Buildings of note in the town centre include the splendid Town Hall with its Corinthian portico, which is set in its own grounds with highly-intricate gold-painted entrance gates, and the Warrington Academy building, which helped earn the town the title of 'Athens of the North'. The academy was built in the era when neither Oxford nor Cambridge would accept anyone who was not a member of the Church of England. Dissenters who were among the leading intellectual lights of their day studied here including Joseph Priestley, who discovered oxygen, and Marat, the French revolutionary. Other names associated with the academy are John Kay, who invented the flying shuttle, and John Howard, the prison reformer. The academy only functioned from 1757 to 1786 and has today been restored to look as it did in those days.

A similar building has been constructed alongside the academy, which is situated just to the north of the Wilderspool bridges over the Mersey near to the statue of Oliver Cromwell. To reach the spot from Central Station, turn left outside the station and continue walking for about ten minutes. From Bank Quay Station turn right and follow the road which parallels the freight-only line which burrows under the station. The town hall is situated between Bank Quay Station and the town centre. Warrington library contains an excellent museum which tells the rich history of the town.

NORTHWICH
by Andrew Macfarlane

Northwich is a town whose prosperity was built on salt and the fascinating history of the industry is told in the unique museum at Weaver Hall. It is situated in London Road beneath the imposing Leftwich viaduct and is open all the year round from Tuesday to Sunday from 2 p.m. to 5 p.m.

Today only one huge salt mine remains at Meadow Bank near Winsford. It has underground roadways covering the area of a town. The salt mine is reputed to be the safest place in Britain and many of the nation's treasures were stored there during the Second World War. The salt provided the basis for the heavy chemical industry which still exists at Winnington and Lostock where soda ash is made from brine and limestone which is brought from the Peak District by rail.

Northwich paid the price for its prosperity and was until relatively recently severely affected by subsidence. Old photographs show the town with buildings leaning at alarming angles. On one famous occasion, a horse and cart vanished into a hole in the road which suddenly opened up. The lesson was learnt that half-timbered buildings resisted subsidence, whereas those of brick simply collapsed into ruins. Several fine half-timbered buildings remain in the town centre. The timber frame allowed the building to be raised on jacks and placed on new foundations as the ground sank.

The sixteenth century Witton Church overlooks the town. It boasts a magnificent ceiling bearing the initials of William Venables who was the then lord of the manor. Carvings from the church are on display in a small open air museum at nearby Vicarsway Park together with other items of local interest.

KNUTSFORD
by Andrew Macfarlane

Knutsford has much to offer both the historian and the tourist. Its two main thoroughfares, Princess Street and King Street, contain many interesting buildings. King Street has several hostelries worthy of note including the elegant eighteenth-century Royal George and the White Lion which dates from the Elizabethan period. The White Bear, situated on the main A50 road, with its thatched roof is of seventeenth-century origin. Knutsford is the Cranford of Mrs Gaskell's novel and the nineteenth-century novelist's grave is contained in the grounds of the Brook Street Unitarian Chapel which is opposite the Chester side of the station on the A537 Macclesfield road. The principal monument to Mrs Gaskell is the early twentieth-century Gaskell Memorial Tower in King Street designed by the architect Richard Harding Watt. Watt was also responsible for the Italianate Ruskin Rooms just off King Street and several houses in Legh Road, off the A537 some ten minutes' walk from the station. These fabulous Italian villas were owned by wealthy industrialists who commuted to 'Cottonopolis' as Manchester was known. One of the houses in Legh Road was occupied by Henry Royce of Rolls-Royce fame.

Knutsford Parish Church, situated just off the A50, was built in 1741 and is a typical example of the Georgian period. The Sessions House opposite was built by Thomas Harrison, who was also responsible for Chester Castle, and dates from 1818. The town allegedly gets its name from King Canute who is said to have forded the River Lily here (it is more likely however that Knut was a ninth-century Danish settler). The king, so the legend goes, met a wedding party as he was shaking sand from his shoes and wished them as many children as there were grains of sand. To this day coloured patterns are made in sand on the pavements of the town on the morning of the May Day procession by men known as 'sanders'. The procession takes place on the first Saturday in May. No mechanically-driven vehicles are allowed and the May Queen and her retinue travel in horse-drawn landaus. Many of the characters in the parade are traditional, including one known as 'Jack in the green' which dates from the time of the druids. A wicker frame is covered in greenery to form a walking tree—the ancient fertility image of the green man. Other characters include Robin Hood and his merry men and a 'village wedding' group recalling the Canute legend.

Tatton Hall, one of the country's most popular stately homes, is some twenty-five minutes' walk from the station. There is a well-signposted entrance to the park at the west end of King Street. The estate is administered by Cheshire County Council on behalf of the National Trust. There are two meres (the Cheshire name for a lake) in the grounds, one of which is due to salt subsidence. The Old Hall has been restored internally to look as it did in the Middle Ages and makes an interesting comparison with the house itself with its sumptuous interior furnishings from the eighteenth century. There are paintings by Van Dyck and Canaletto as well as furniture by Gillow. The Tenants Hall houses a museum of the late Lord Egerton's hunting trophies and no. M1, the first car to be registered in Cheshire. Finally, do not miss the famous Japanese Garden.

FURTHER INFORMATION

Tourist Boards

North West Tourist Board, The Last Drop Village, Bromley Cross, Bolton, Lancashire, BL7 9PZ. Tel. 0204–591511

East Midlands Tourist Board, Exchequergate, Lincoln, Lincolnshire, LN2 1PZ. Tel. 0522–531521

Heart of England Tourist Board, 2–4 Trinity Street, Worcester, WR1 2PW. Tel. 0905–613132

All three tourist boards publish annual guides which give details of all places of interest and selected accommodation. These guides are obtainable from the respective boards (as are a number of more detailed local guides), from tourist information offices and from many bookshops. The telephone numbers of some of the more important tourist information offices are:

The Crescent, Buxton. Tel. 0298–5106
Castlefield Visitors' Centre, 330 Deansgate, Castlefield, Manchester M3 4FN.
    Tel. 061–832–4244
Town Hall, Chester. Tel. 0244–313126 or 324324, after office hours 0244–
    349026
Earle Street, Crewe. Tel. 0270–583191
Central Library, The Wardwick, Derby. Tel. 0332–290664
City Museum, Bethesda Street, Hanley, Stoke-on-Trent. Tel. 0782–285910
Council Offices, Toft Road, Knutsford. Tel. 0565–2611
29 Lime Street, Liverpool. Tel. 051–709–3631
Atlantic Pavilion, Albert Dock, Liverpool. Tel. 051–708–8854
Macclesfield. Tel. 0625–21955
Town Hall Extension, Lloyd Street, Manchester. Tel. 061–234–3157 and 3158
The Pavilion, Matlock Bath. Tel. 0629–55082
Marine Promenade, New Brighton. Tel. 051–638–7144
Town Hall Extension, Union Street, Sheffield. Tel. 0742–734671
Ancient High House, Greengate Street, Stafford. Tel. 0785–40204
Civic Offices, Riverside, Stafford. Tel. 0785–223181
1 Glebe Street, Stoke-on-Trent. Tel. 0782–411222
Warrington. Tel. 0925–36501

Maps

A good map is essential for the country walks suggested in this book and is
desirable for cycle rides. Ordnance Survey publish maps of various scales, each
series suited for particular purposes. For details, write to Information and Public
Enquiries, Ordnance Survey, Romsey Road, Maybush, Southampton, SO9 4DH.
Other useful maps are in the National Series published by John Bartholomew &
Sons Ltd., Duncan Street, Edinburgh, EH9 1TA.

Rail Information

British Rail publish a passenger timetable for the whole country, of over 1400
pages. This is issued in May and September each year, with subsequent sup-
plements, and can be bought at staffed stations and booksellers. Free timetable
booklets and leaflets are also available for individual lines or groups of lines at
staffed stations, as are leaflets on the carriage of bicycles by train. Local rail
information can be obtained by dialling the following:

Buxton 0298–2101
Chester 0244–40170
Crewe 0270–255245
Derby 0332–32051
Liverpool 051–709–9696

Manchester 061–832–8353
Sheffield 0742–726411
Shrewsbury 0743–64041
Stoke-on-Trent 0782–411411
Warrington 0925–32245

Steam Train Operators

The Dinting Railway Centre Limited, Dinting Lane, Glossop, Derbyshire.
    Tel. 04574–5596. Further information from Mr K. J. Tait, 73 Derby Road,
    Heaton Moor, Stockport, Cheshire SK4 4NG.
Foxfield Steam Railway, Caverswall Road Station, Blythe Bridge, Stoke-on-
    Trent. Tel. 0782–396210 (weekends only). Further information from Mrs L.
    J. Reed, Secretary, Foxfield Light Railway Society Limited, 63 Maythorne
    Road, Blurton, Stoke-on-Trent. Tel. 0782–314532.
Greater Manchester Museum of Science and Industry, Liverpool Road,
    Manchester M3 4JP. Tel. 061–832–2244.
North Staffordshire Railway Limited, Cheddleton Station, Cheddleton, Leek,
    Staffordshire.

PeakRail plc, Buxton Midland Station, Buxton, Derbyshire SK17 6AQ.
  Tel. 0298–79898 or (Matlock) 0629–580381.

Bus information
The deregulation of bus services has brought with it constant changes in bus routes and timetables in many areas and intending passengers are strongly advised to check services with the individual operator before travelling. In addition, in metropolitan areas such as Greater Manchester and Merseyside the passenger transport executives act as clearing houses for bus information from all operators and they can inform passengers of the particular operator(s) for each service. Cheshire County Council also produce timetables for all bus services within the county. Useful addresses are:

Greater Manchester Passenger Transport Executive, PO Box 429, Portland
  Street, Manchester M60 1HX. Timetable enquiries 061–228–7811.
Merseyside Passenger Transport Executive, 24 Hatton Garden, Liverpool,
  Merseyside L3 2AN. Timetable enquiries 051–236–7676.
Transportation Unit, Cheshire County Council, Backford Hall, Chester CH1
  6EA. Tel. 0244–602424.

Bus operators at time of going to press:
Chester City Transport Limited, Station Road, Chester CH1 3AD. Tel. 0244–
  47452.
Chesterfield Borough Transport Limited, Stonegravels Depot, Sheffield Road,
  Chesterfield, Derbyshire S41 7JW. Tel. 0246–276666.
Crosville Motor Services Limited, Crane Wharf, Chester CH1 4SQ. Tel. 0244–
  381515. (Crewe) 0270–212256.
Derby City Transport Limited, Victoria Street, Derby, Derbyshire. Tel. 0332–
  754433.
Devaway Travel, Broughton, Mills Road, Bretton, Clwyd. Tel. 0244–661195.
East Midland Motor Services Limited (Mansfield), New Street, Chesterfield,
  Derbyshire S40 2LQ. Tel. 0246–275432.
Greater Manchester Buses Limited, 2 Devonshire Street North, Ardwick,
  Manchester M12 6JS. Tel. 061–273–5341.
Halton Borough Transport Limited, Moor Lane, Widnes, Cheshire. Tel. 051–
  423–3333.
Merseybus, Liverpool, Merseyside. Tel. 051–254–1616.
Midland Red North (Chaserider), Charlton Street, Wellington, Telford,
  Shropshire. Tel. 0952–223767. (Stafford) Tel. 0785–42997.
PMT Limited, 33 Woodhouse Street, Stoke-on-Trent ST4 1EQ. Tel. 0782–
  747000.
Silver Service Travel, 12a Bank Road, Matlock, Derbyshire. Tel. 0629–580212.
Smiths Shearings Limited, Victoria Mill, Miry Lane, Wigan, Lancashire WN3
  4AG. Tel. 0942–46254.
South Yorkshire's Transport, Sheffield, South Yorkshire. Tel. 0742–755655.
Stevenson's of Uttoxeter Limited, The Office, Brooklands, Spath, Uttoxeter,
  Staffordshire. Tel. 0889–562131.
SUT Limited, Pond Street, Sheffield, South Yorkshire. Tel. 0742–739966.
Trent Motor Traction Company Limited, PO Box 35, Uttoxeter New Road,
  Derby DE3 3NJ. Tel. 0332–292200.
Warrington Borough Transport Limited, Wilderspool Causeway, Warrington,
  Cheshire WA4 6PT. Tel. 0925–34296.

Timetables for these and other operators' services can often also be obtained from public libraries, bus stations and tourist information centres.

COME AND JOIN US!

The Railway Development Society is a national, voluntary, independent body which campaigns for better rail services, for both passengers and freight, and greater use of rail transport.

It publishes books and papers, holds meetings and exhibitions, sometimes runs special trains and generally endeavours to put the case for rail to politicians, civil servants, commerce and industry, and the public at large; as well as feeding users' comments and suggestions to British Rail management and unions.

Membership is open to all who are in general agreement with the aims of the society and subscriptions are:

Standard rate: **£7.50**

Reduced rate (for pensioners, full-time students): **£4**

Families: **£7.50** plus **£1** for each member of the household

Special rates also apply for corporate bodies.

Write to the Membership Secretary, Mr F. J. Hastilow, 49 Irnham Road, Four Oaks, Sutton Coldfield, West Midlands B74 2TQ.

The North West branch covers most of the area covered by this book, the North Midlands branch covers Derbyshire (except High Peak) and the Midlands branch covers Staffordshire. The addresses of the relevant secretaries are:

North West branch: Mr A. D. MacFarlane, 16 Willow Green, Knutsford,
    Cheshire WA16 6AX. Tel. 0565–53554.

North Midlands branch: Mr R. M. Goodall, Albemarle Cottage, Kirklington
    Road, Eakring, Nottingham NG22 0DA.

Midlands branch: Mr R. J. Smith, 27 Moreland Croft, Minworth, Sutton
    Coldfield, West Midlands B76 8XZ. Tel. 021–351–5588.

In addition there are several local line users' groups in the area covered, most of whom are affiliated to the Railway Development Society:

High Peak Railway Passengers' Association (Manchester–Buxton line): Mr E.
    Bradbury, Kinder, 38 Horderns Road, Chapel-en-le-Frith SK12 6TB.
    Tel. 0298–813163.

Hope Valley Rail Users' Group: Dr H. Porteous, 115 Wollaton Road, Sheffield
    S17 4LF. Tel. 0742–366674.

Mid Cheshire Rail Users' Association (Manchester–Northwich–Chester line):

Mr A. D. MacFarlane, 16 Willow Green, Knutsford, Cheshire WA16 6AX.
    Tel. 0565–53554.

Wirral Transport Users' Association: Mr A. Tilston, 17 Poulton Road,
    Bebington, Wirral, Merseyside L63 9LA. Tel. 051–334–5546.

Wrexham–Birkenhead Rail Users' Association: Mr G. Tolliday, 3 Southbank,
    Oxton, Birkenhead, Merseyside L43 5UP. Tel. 051–652–9898.

ISBN 0–7117–0429–5
©Railway Development Society 1989
Published by Jarrold Colour Publications, Norwich
Printed in Great Britain. 1/89